THE SMARTER

EXIT

A strategic plan to scale and exit your business

CLIFF SPOLANDER

Foreword by Jessen James

www.businessoptics.co.uk

THE SMARTER EXIT
A strategic plan to scale and exit your business

ISBN: 978-1-9163505-2-6 (paperback)
ISBN: 978-1-9163505-3-3 (ePub)
Also available for Kindle

Cover art design: Luke Benjamin@lukebenjamindesigns
Layout & pre-press: Lighthouse24

Acknowledgement

I want to thank my wife, Susie, and our children, Reuben and Phoebe – it sure has been a journey! I know this book would not have been possible were it not for your love and support over the years. Thank you for being my rock and my motivation!

Then to all you hard working entrepreneurs who serve others. I hope this book will help and guide you. It is my sincere prayer that I would have served you in some small way along your journey. Finish strong and make the most of every day!

THE SMARTER EXIT

Contents

Foreword

In a world where business has become ever more uncertain, it is essential that business owners bulletproof their financial futures and protect their hard-earned investments. However, the challenge for most owners is that when they start their business, they give themselves a job. They become self-employed; they employ themselves. Whilst that may be the dream for many business owners, the challenge of self-employment is that there is rarely a retirement plan.

What do I mean by this?

You have given yourself a job with a boss who is usually too hard on themselves, rarely takes any time off and cannot be replaced. That becomes a problem if life throws you a curve ball and you, as the business owner, cannot work. What happens to your business? I would guess that, if you are like most entrepreneurs nowadays who do not leverage processes, systems and people to support you and your business, chances are that your business will fall apart.

Let's dig deeper…What would happen to the people who rely on your business: your team members, your employees, your family, your children – those that rely on the company's turnover and your income? What would happen to your mortgage, your rent, your bills, your car, your children's schooling, food on your table…the list goes on and on. When we think of it like this, it becomes a real concern.

However, there is help available to plan for those concerns and avoid the worry that many business owners face, and that help comes in the form of this book. This book is written by a very special individual. I have had the pleasure of knowing and working with Cliff Spolander for some time now. Having trained tens of thousands of entrepreneurs across the world, every now and then a hidden gem turns up. That hidden gem is Cliff. This man not only has the experience to help business owners like you create a solid retirement plan and exit their businesses successfully in the future, but has been there and done that himself, and has trained and consulted hundreds of entrepreneurs, just like you.

Not only do I believe he is the go-to person to help you with this, but he also has a heart of gold. This man doesn't only want you to become a better entrepreneur; he wants you to become a better human being – a better father, mother, sibling, spouse – an all-round better individual.

This book contains all the tools, strategies and information you need in order to bulletproof your financial future, set your business on the path to success and structure your company to thrive, whether you are there or not. When you implement the principles and advice in this book, you will find yourself in the ideal position with options:

Option one: You can sell your business.

Option two: You can reduce the hours you work in your business without having to worry about the financial impact.

Option three: You can hire somebody else to run that business for you.

Whether you have been in business for many years or you are just starting out, you need to start thinking about how you will exit your business *right now*. In the great words of Dr Stephen Covey, "Start with the end in mind". My advice to you would be to start with the end in mind, know exactly what you want, learn how to get there and live your life on your terms.

Jessen James
Award-winning public speaker and CEO of Global Success Ltd

The 5-Year Business Plan

THE IDEA AND PURPOSE behind this methodology is simple: to get you and your business exit ready within five years, irrespective of whether you plan to exit in 10-, 20- or 30-years' time. This, of course, doesn't mean that you have to exit in five years' time, but it means you will be ready.

Why Be Exit Ready?

It is true that many smaller businesses will probably never sell, but the owner will still have to exit at some point. Everyone will have to exit whether they like it or not. (This will be covered when we look at the 7 Ds later in the book.)

The question I would like to ask you is: Do you want to maximise the return for all the hard work and time you have ploughed into the business, or do you simply want to throw it all away? I hope that most business owners reading this will see the folly in investing and working in a business for many years just to see it disappear, with no return on investment, when it's time to stop working in your business.

Therefore, I would like to encourage you to start planning your exit as soon as possible. It doesn't matter the size of your business or what your future plans or aspirations may be. Exit planning is not just about selling your business, although selling is one way of exiting a business. It is about exiting your business successfully – and by 'successfully', I mean ensuring all your business, personal and financial goals are met, providing you with choices and the opportunity to live the lifestyle to which you aspire. The key word here is 'choices' because, all too often, I meet with business owners looking to exit who have no choices, so they are forced down a particular route – normally one that they did not plan and do not want to go down.

In this book, I will show you how to create and implement an exit strategy for you and your business and I will explain the steps involved in helping you achieve a successful exit.

Why Five Years?

There are three reasons why I recommend a five-year plan:

1. Life is uncertain.
2. Exiting doesn't happen quickly.
3. A plan gives buyers a better picture.

Life is uncertain. No one knows what is around the corner. By getting your business, personal life, and financial plans in order, you will be prepared to exit your business if your life changes in any way. Statistics show that around 50% of business owners will be forced to exit their business at some point. This is staggering – one out of two business owners will have no choice as to when they exit. Now, this could be for a variety of reasons, but the reasons I come across most often are illness, injury, a change in family circumstances or death.

Unfortunately, I have seen first-hand the consequences of business owners not being ready. Essentially, they are stuck between a rock and a hard place. On the one hand, they need the time to deal with whatever personal problems they have, and on the other hand, they have the finances and the business to contend with. They need the business to be sold for a particular amount, but if the business is not exit ready, they will not get the valuation they are seeking. So, they are left to choose between time or money; they either have time with their family but take a financial hit or spend more time in the business to improve its financial value but have less time with their family. This is not an easy choice to make, so it is my mission to make sure that business owners, who are the backbone of the country's economy, have better and wider choices than those I am currently seeing.

Exiting doesn't happen quickly. It takes a substantial amount of time to get a business exit ready. It is not like selling a house, where you can make it attractive to a buyer by tidying the garden and giving the house a lick of paint. Remember: You still need to run the business whilst you work on preparing it for exit. Therefore, the five-year timescale gives you sufficient time to realign the business and prepare it for exit, especially when it comes to preparing for the due diligence phase – a critical phase in the sale of a business that can make or break a deal – which you'll learn about in this book.

A plan gives buyers a better picture. From a buyer's perspective, what they want to see are positive, sustainable trends because this will add confidence as well as value to the business. Because buyers will typically want to see at least two to three years of financial accounts, the five-year preparation period gives the owner time to accrue adequate accounts to show a buyer what is really happening within the business and what is realistically achievable in the future.

Very often, I see a business for sale where the sales and profit have remained fairly static over the years but then the turnover and/or profit have suddenly increased in the last six to 12 months. This represents when the owner has conducted some massive sales and marketing activity or cost-cutting exercise and then uses that growth to justify the value of the business. In most cases, if not all cases, buyers see right through that because no one knows whether that growth in turnover or profit is sustainable.

The plan over the first five years is to make your business attractive and saleable and to create a personal plan that prepares you for your life post exit and ensures you are financially prepared. Should something unexpected happen, you and your business are ready for exit. However, at this point in time, it is very unlikely that your business commands the valuation you require to be in a financial position to retire. Therefore, you will need to continue to run and scale the business, using this Business By Design methodology, until you choose or are forced to exit. As stated before: exit planning is simply good business strategy.

About Me

In over 20 years of being in business, I have started, bought and sold businesses in the retail, education, health and construction sectors. I have had the privilege of franchising a business and licensing another in five countries. Over the years, I've learnt some tough lessons, made mistakes, lost money, and, at times, was too naive. I have experienced the highs and the joys of owning my own business, and I also know how intensive a start-up can be due to the time, energy, commitment and sacrifice that is needed to make a business successful.

During my career, my experience of being both a business seller and a business buyer has given me unique insight into how it feels to be on both sides of the fence, what each party is looking to achieve, the frustrations they experience and what it takes to make a deal work in order to get it over the line.

All these experiences, both good and bad, have formed who I am today as a business owner, as a business buyer and in my advisory work. It is this wealth of experience that I want to share with you in this book: my own personal experiences, as well as those I have observed in other business owners. This array of experiences has inspired me to create Business By Design, a methodology using a proven process to help business owners navigate their way to owning an exit-ready business. Integrated into this methodology are bespoke tools and procedures that I have created to provide the Clarity and Control required for a successful exit.

It is my intention to help you make the most of your business, your opportunity, and at the same time, to help you achieve this seemingly unachievable 'work-life balance'. I am not saying the journey will be easy. As I'm sure you will agree, being in business isn't easy – it's the path less travelled. But I want those who step out and undertake this journey to learn from my mistakes and the observations I have made over the past two decades so that their journey may be a little easier.

Over the years, when looking to acquire businesses, I have examined over a thousand companies. I have had to kiss a lot of frogs to find that elusive 'princess'. The question I ask myself is, 'Why has it been so difficult? Why are there so many frogs?' Having spoken with owners and having seen the same results time and time again, I have uncovered some common reasons I have identified through many, if not all, of the companies I have examined.

So, let's start unpacking these common reasons, beginning with a story.

A Tale of Two Owners

It was the best of times; it was the worst of times…

The thrill and excitement of running your own business followed by frustration, disappointment and the harsh reality that this journey on which you've chosen to embark is not an easy one. Isn't this what most business owners face on a monthly, weekly, sometimes daily basis?

We give so much of ourselves to our businesses – our time, our energy, our sacrifice, our money, our life – that, at the end of the day, we all hope to get a return for that investment. Otherwise, what's the point?

We must face the reality that, one day, we will have to leave our company for one reason or another. For some, it will be out of choice whilst others will be forced to leave due to unforeseen circumstances such as death, illness, etc. When we leave our company, whether by choice or not, the business should and must produce a return for the commitment that has been invested. However, sadly, for most business owners, this is rarely the case.

Let me share with you the story of two business owners. Their stories may resonate with some of you, but for others, this may be a new realisation.Let me share with you the story of two business owners. Their stories may resonate with some of you, but for others, this may be a new realisation.

Bill's Story

Bill was an incredibly talented welder and designer. He started his Bill was an incredibly talented welder and designer. He started his career working for a large international company in the design and manufacture of racing car parts, including Formula One and Formula Two. When this industry started to move away from using metal and towards using stronger, lighter composite materials, the company chose to close this part of the business down. Bill saw this as his opportunity to start his own business and use his skills in other areas, which he did with incredible success. He grew his business and, at the height of his success, employed 16 people with a seven-figure turnover.

Bill was great at what he did – all things welding – but really struggled when it came to the business end of running the company. He found it easier to stay on the shop floor and preferred designing, building and training his staff. He didn't focus on where or how the business was performing.

When I met Bill to discuss buying his business, he was tired, worn-out and stressed. Over the past 30 years, the business had gone from making sales of just over a million pounds to barely making six figures. He had two part-time members of staff, both well past retirement age, and as he was approaching his late sixties himself, Bill wanted to sell the business and move on. His aim was to take the money made from the sale of the business and use that to help fund his retirement, including a relocation to the South-West coast.

When we met for the first time, Bill's business had already been on the market for over a year, having had several interested parties, none of whom took it any further. After looking at the company's financials, it became apparent that he was in serious financial trouble. Profits were trending down year-on-year and now sat below £10,000. He had incurred debt of over £60,000, £35,000 of which was owed to the non-payment of rent for his office and warehouse.

Despite all of this, Bill was still very optimistic about selling his business for around £180,000 because that was what he felt the business to be worth and also what his business broker had told him.

I felt it only right to be honest with him and explain that his business was unsaleable for several reasons:

1. The business had too much debt.
2. There had been no capital investment for well over 15 years.
3. His staff were due to retire in the next 12 to 18 months.

4. There were no systems or processes in place, either on the shop floor or in the office.

5. The real deal-killer was that everything revolved around him; he held all the knowledge, experience and skill. Without Bill, unless someone had the same skillset as him, there would be no guarantee that even a fraction of what he had at that time could be replicated, let alone to the extent he'd had at the height of his business.

Bill did – or didn't do – several things to land his business in this 'unsaleable' situation. These were things that I see a lot of other business owners do, all of which will be discussed in the chapters of this book. The major issue for Bill was that he had remained the central figure of his business and, because he'd remained the expert 'worker' and hadn't focused on developing the business by becoming his company's CEO, his business couldn't operate without him. The other major contributing factor was that he'd never planned for the future. He'd never made a strategy for exiting his business. He'd missed the boat when the company was making over a million pounds in sales in that he chose to keep the business rather than look to sell it. Later, as his energy levels waned, so too did the company's sales and overall value. Being unaware of the need to look ahead and see beyond the horizon had prevented Bill from acting sooner when he could have achieved a healthy return. His lack of strategic planning likely resulted in him not achieving the return he was seeking.

At the time of writing, 2.5 years later, Bill's business has just been taken off the market as, sadly, he passed away in November of 2021 at age 69. He had been unable to achieve his dream of retiring to the South-West coast to spend time with his family because he had no choice other than to keep working.

Sarah's Story

Sarah had a student lettings company. She was young, ambitious and driven, and, on the surface, her business was doing exceptionally well. Within four years, her revenue was almost hitting the seven-figure mark, with a very healthy net profit.

Sarah had a small team consisting of a personal assistant (her mother) who helped out with the finances and other office administration and a part-time staff member who carried out inspections and viewings. It was a slick operation but, crucially, Sarah was at the centre of the business doing a lot of the face-to-face work. She was well-known and respected by tenants and landlords alike.

Despite this growing and seemingly successful business, Sarah wanted to sell. Given the growth of the business and her age, which was 34 at the time, I was very curious as to why she was selling. It transpired that she had been diagnosed with an illness and needed to sell the business before she became too weak and sick. She was hoping to achieve around £400,000 but was willing to accept an offer of £250,000 if it was paid up front.

Unfortunately, despite the impressive figures, her business model was not sustainable. She was not simply a letting agent, *she was the tenant*. Her company rented the properties from the landlords, guaranteeing them a rental income for a two-year period in exchange for a reduced rent; then she would sublet the rooms to students and pocket the difference. Because she was effectively the tenant, her business was liable for all the rent for that two-year period, whether or not the properties were occupied. Thus, the total liability on her balance sheet was around half a million pounds. It was a high-risk but high-reward business model; however, an unexpected event, such as a global pandemic, would potentially cripple the company – which ended up happening.

Even without the pandemic, the debt that any acquirer would be signing up for would have been over half a million pounds. Any change in the company's tenancy agreement with the current landlords would probably cause them to go elsewhere. It was a high-risk model that had worked for Sarah but was not necessarily conducive to creating a saleable business.

I'm not saying the business model was wrong; it was a perfectly sound model, provided life didn't throw any curveballs. Unfortunately, in Sarah's case, life did throw the curveballs, and the business model could not withstand them.

Bill and Sarah's stories are not unique. I have had many more encounters with business owners looking to sell their companies but finding themselves in difficulty due to the way that their businesses had been set up and managed, sometimes over many years. This is something that I'm coming across all too often; too many owners are forced to sell their businesses sooner than they'd anticipated, sometimes due to being completely worn out or stressed; disagreements between business partners; or injury, illness, or death.

None of us know what's around the corner and what life will throw at us, but we can prepare as best we can. As you read through this book, I will explain what you can do to prepare both yourself and your business for the future so you can be in the ideal exit-ready position, whether you need to exit within three months or 30 years. Statistics show that around 50% of business owners will be forced to exit their businesses before they'd intended, demonstrating how important it is to always be exit ready.

This book will guide you through how best to prepare both yourself and your business so that you can be as ready as possible to exit your business successfully, whether it should become suddenly necessary or fits within your planned timescale. Doing this will help get you to a point where all your hard work, time, effort, money and sacrifice pays off and you can move on to the next chapter of your life, safe in the knowledge that you have made the most of your opportunity.

To clarify, getting your business exit ready does not mean you have to exit your business. It simply means you are in a position to exit should you want to or if you are forced to by an unexpected turn of events.

The Book's Setup

This book is split into two parts:

Part One

This first part aims to persuade all business owners that starting to create an exit plan is essential, all-important and high-priority. In my work as a certified exit planning advisor, I work with many business owners. The problem I find is that every one of them needs to be exit ready, but 99% of them don't want to put in the effort to get the measures in place. This is because they do not see exit planning as something they need to do now, but rather as something they can leave for another time in the future. Therefore, the purpose of part one of this book is to highlight the importance of creating your exit plan today, not leaving it until you want or need to exit, when it may be too late.

Part one supplies a variety of reasons to get you motivated to act. In chapters 1 and 2, you'll encounter the grim reasons why you'd better get started on making that exit plan. You'll become well informed of the harsh realities that most businesses face when they make an unplanned exit or are forced to exit without an exit plan in place. Chapters 3 and 4 show you how creating an exit plan today will not only benefit you in the future when you eventually decide to exit, but also help to drive and scale your business, creating balance and satisfaction across all major parts of your life in the interim.

Part Two

By the end of part one, you should be eager, perhaps even overeager, to start implementing the strategies for making your business exit ready, which brings us to part two. The second part of the book focuses on the methodology of exit planning: the raw ingredients for creating and implementing an exit strategy and the steps you can take to gain the Clarity, Control and Consistency to finally Complete your goal – to exit successfully – when you need to make that exit. This process is extremely focused and strategic; it is designed to get you from where you now – wherever that may be – to the place of exit readiness. It takes into consideration the three key elements required to make this happen: business, personal and financial plans. Through this methodology, I will show you how to move from an 'owner-centric' business model to a 'value-centric' business model.

This Stabilise-Systemise-Scale Process is known to bring Clarity, Control and Consistency to every business owner. By following the unique Business By Design methodology in this book, you'll feel more confident and supported to take the next steps in preparing your business for exit and to prepare yourself for whatever life may hold.

It is my goal and passion to see every business owner become exit ready so that they are able to enjoy the rewards of their hard work, while they are still running their business and once they have moved on. More importantly, I want every owner to be as prepared as possible for any unexpected events that life may throw at them, to have options and be able to remain on the front foot.

Why It's Critical to Be Exit Ready

PART ONE SUPPLIES a variety of reasons to get you motivated to act. In chapters 1 and 2, you'll encounter the grim reasons why you'd better get started on making that exit plan, well before you plan on exiting. Chapters 3 and 4 show you how creating an exit plan today benefits you not only when you finally do exit, but in the interim as well – on a daily basis across your business, personal and financial life.

By the end of part one, expect to be impatient to get your business exit ready!

CHAPTER 1
The Need for Exit Planning

As STATED IN THE INTRODUCTION, the aim of part one is to convince you, the business owner, that it is critical, crucial, absolutely necessary to begin creating your exit strategy today. Whether you plan on exiting in one month, one year, six years, or 20 years, you need to start planning your exit strategy: it is never too early. Owners of small- to medium-sized enterprises (SMEs) are the target audience for this book, and I want to add that this includes businesses with no employees – "one-man bands" – as well as businesses whose owners consider their company unsaleable. All of these types of business owners must begin planning their exit strategy today. You are all included in my urgent message, although your type of exit strategy will vary. This chapter is all about understanding exit planning – what it is, what it means to be exit ready and the consequences of not being exit ready. We will also uncover the three main reasons as to why most business owners do not have an exit strategy in place.

The Current Landscape

Before we delve into exit planning, let's take a step back and consider what part the small- and medium-sized businesses play within the UK market and the realities that we, as business owners, face. (I include myself in this 'we' because I too am an owner of several small businesses, so everything I am writing also applies to me and my businesses.) We need to understand our landscape so we know what market forces are at play and how best to operate within our surroundings.

The Current Landscape

1,415,980 UK Businesses

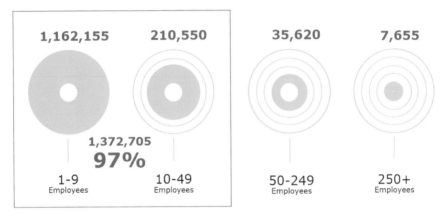

Office for National Statistics 2021

The statistics from the Office for National Statistics (UK) 2021 shown above may change over time, but broadly speaking, it is the relative percentages that I'd like to share with you. This will give you a good idea of how much the SME market dominates the business landscape within the UK. There are approximately 1.4 million businesses employing more than one person in the UK. Companies employing one to 50 people account for over 97% of the UK market.

Therefore, looking at the landscape as well as the demographics, especially over the next five to 25 years, we will see the Baby Boomer generation retire, coupled with the Gen X and Millennials starting to think about their future. With this scenario, supply will outstrip demand, creating a buyers' market. If selling your business is one of your aims and part of your exit plan, you need to stand out from the crowd and attract as many buyers as possible. As you'll see over the course of this book, creating an exit strategy now – even if you are years away from exiting – will make your business stand out from the crowd and help establish the sale value you are aiming to achieve.

The Current Reality

Start-Up Statistics for an SME Business Owner

Life is not easy for an SME owner; the odds are stacked against you from the beginning. According to the Office for National Statistics (UK), the following are the statistics regarding the failure rate of SMEs:

- About 10% fail in their first year.
- About 60% of small businesses fail by the fifth year.

From the averages based upon the survival rate of new enterprises in the United Kingdom from 2007 to 2017, we can see that:

- About 90% of businesses *with employees* will survive their first year in business.
- About 75% of businesses *with employees* will survive their second year in business.
- About 40% of businesses *with employees* will survive their fifth year in business.
- About 30% of businesses *with employees* will survive their tenth year in business.

	Year 1	Year 2	Year 3	Year 4	Year 5	Year 10
Survival Rates	91.25%	74.11%	59.43%	49.98%	42.67%	33.12%

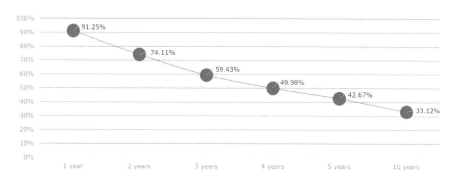

—SME Survival Rates

Office for National Statistics (UK)

According to Investopedia, the four most common reasons why small businesses fail come down to: (1) a lack of capital; (2) poor management; (3) inadequate business planning; and (4) cash flow problems.

However, for early-stage businesses, there are many more than these four reasons as to why they don't survive, as indicated by CB Insights. In analysing a number of start-ups to find the reasons why those businesses failed according to their owners, CB Insights found the following:

- 42% of small businesses failed because there was no market need for their services or products.
- 29% failed because they ran out of cash.
- 23% failed because they did not have the right team running the business.
- 19% were outcompeted.
- 18% failed because of pricing and cost issues.
- 17% failed because of a poor product offering.
- 17% failed because they lacked a business model.
- 14% failed because of poor marketing.
- 14% failed because they ignored their customers.

Why am I supplying you with these morbid failure statistics? To convince you that even if by chance your business seems to be doing fine now, failure happens all the time and for a number of reasons, none of which include the owner planning for it. Indeed, there is the familiar saying: 'Failing to plan is planning to fail'. Because failing happens often and quickly, business owners must be exit ready at all times. We must have a plan in place today, now, so that down the road, if life throws a curveball at us or at our business, we are prepared to handle it and make the most of all that we've put into our business thus far. Even if a business is one of the lucky 30% that make it to their tenth business birthday, the owner must plan for the future so that their exit may be successful, whether this is a sale or a different type of exit.

The Exit Statistics for an SME Business Owner

A Business Optics Survey conducted from 2010-2019 looked at companies employing between one and 50 people and estimated that out of the 1.3 million businesses:

- More than 90% aren't sellable in their current condition.
- For those that are for sale, less than 20% will sell.
- For those that do sell, less than 5% will sell for what the owner expected.

To make matters worse, it is estimated that around 50% of business owners will be forced to exit their business unexpectedly due to ill health or a change in their personal circumstances.

So, not only are the odds of survival stacked against us whilst we run our business, when it comes to selling when we do exit, there is a less than one in five chance of actually selling it and an even smaller chance of selling it for the amount that we need to sell it for.

Let's talk about what the drivers behind these statistics are and what can be done about them.

Exit success hinges around a business owner's knowledge of what exit planning is as well as their understanding of how to create an exit strategy. As we go through this book, we will unpack these two concepts and develop your knowledge and understanding to put you in the best position possible for exit success.

What Exit Planning Is

There are two very common misconceptions when it comes to exit planning:

- Misconception 1: You should start planning your exit *when* you want to sell.
- Misconception 2: You only need an exit strategy *if* you want to sell.

Let's look at each in turn.

Misconception 1: *You should start planning your exit when you want to sell.*

Many business owners start exit planning far too late. By the time they want or need to exit their business, there is very little time to get the business ready for sale. This either forces them to sell their business for a lot less than what they were hoping for or close the business down. Due to financial reasons, some owners may be forced to continue working in their business.

Misconception 2: *You only need an exit strategy if you want to sell.*

There are a lot of 'one-person-with-a-laptop' businesses. The typical remarks I hear from owners of these businesses include the following:

- 'Well, it's just me and my laptop. The business is not worth anything to a buyer'.
- 'I'm never going to sell. I will keep working for as long as I can'.
- 'My business is too reliant upon me and only I can run the business. No one would buy it'.

It is true that many microbusinesses or "one-man band" businesses will probably never sell, but the owner will have to exit at some point, whether they like it or not and whether they have planned for it or not. Not all exit plans include a sale, but even still, all business owners must plan their exit. For a micro-business owner who will have to exit someday, the question is: Do they want to maximise the return for all the hard work and time they have ploughed into the business, or will they simply throw it away? I would hope that most business owners would see the folly in investing and working in their business for many years to just throw it all away. While some micro-businesses do carry some value and are saleable (for instance, being able to sell their client base to another business looking to expand), those that aren't saleable should still get exit ready today by becoming tax efficient in order to build up a pension pot for the owner's retirement. You can't build up a pot of any substance in the space of only the year or six months before you have decided to retire; you build that pot through an exit strategy that has been put into place many years before you actually exit, something we'll look at in later chapters.

In the chapters that follow, I propose that no matter the size of your business or what your plans or aspirations may be, the strategies in this book will work for you. Exit planning is not just about selling your business; it is about exiting your business *successfully* – and by 'successfully' I mean ensuring all your business, personal and financial goals are met.

Exit Readiness

What does it mean to be 'exit ready', and why should you care anyway?

Let me give you an example that will bring home the importance and the reality of being exit ready.

A business owner in his late forties had a well-established business producing a decent living for him and his family. Due to his age, he felt he was a good 10 to 15 years away from selling his business and was content with sticking to the status quo.

The level of his pension was not where he wanted it to be, but as he still had a few years left to work, the shortfall would be made up by pension contributions made by his business and other assets he had.

Unfortunately, he was diagnosed with an aggressive form of liver cancer and was given only months to live. In the desperate rush to get all his affairs in order, he and his wife spent the rest of their time together sorting out all the logistics, finances and the business. This was precious time that he could have spent enjoying being with his wife and three children. It was not long before he passed away, and the bitter regret of his wife and children was not being in a position where all this 'stuff' was organised and in order. As his business was not exit ready and was still heavily reliant upon him, it could not be sold. All the years of hard work and sacrifice – time away from his family – had gone to waste. Additionally, the several people he employed had their lives turned upside down and they all had to find new jobs.

I am not telling you this story to make you feel depressed (I understand that this example doesn't make for easy reading) but to emphasise the reality of not being exit ready. Planning your exit does not necessarily mean you'll have to exit your business now or even at some point in the future; it simply means that if life throws you a curveball, if someone approaches you with an interest to buy your business or if you simply decide you've had enough, you'll be able to respond accordingly. Being prepared will allow you to grab an opportunity, should it arise and, in less opportune circumstances, will reduce the impact on your family and those with whom you work.

Being exit ready is about being ready for whatever is around the corner. It is about creating options instead of dead ends.

An EPI study found that 75% of business owners surveyed within one year of exit profoundly regretted the decision.
—The Exit Planning Institute (EPI)

By not having an exit strategy in place well ahead of when you actually make the exit, you risk becoming one of those owners who, like those in the EPI survey mentioned above, regretted their exit decision.

The whole acquisition process is fraught with uncertainty: a deal may not complete; the offer could change at the last minute; your personal circumstances could change; or the deal structure may be modified, forcing you to accept a lower amount on completion or a longer deferred term. If there are any underlying problems within the business, they too could reduce its overall value.

Therefore, by not preparing the business properly, you could put yourself and your family at risk financially. As shown already in this chapter, by looking at the current landscape, you'll see the odds are stacked against SME owners. But, by following the proven Business By Design methodology, which is explained in part two of this book, you not only give yourself the very best chance of having the business you always dreamed of, but you set yourself up to be as prepared as possible for all eventualities.

In order to really cement your awareness and increase your motivation to pursue part two of this book – the 'how' of planning the most appropriate exit strategy for your type of business – let's continue looking at reasons why it is so critical to do so. This brings us to the next chapter, which is about how things play out when a business owner is not exit ready but forced to exit anyway.

Chapter 1 Takeaways

- This is a buyers' market.
- The odds, as they stand now, are against SME owners.
- Don't leave exit planning for when it is too late.
- Every business owner needs an exit strategy, whether they plan to sell or not.
- Exit success hinges on a business owner's knowledge and understanding of exit planning.
- Preparation is key. No one knows what is around the corner.

CHAPTER 2

Not Ready? Uh-Oh...
It's Going to Be a Rough Ride

As PREVIOUSLY EXPLAINED, throughout my years of looking to acquire businesses, I have examined over a thousand companies, and it has been through my conversations with owners that I have seen first-hand the consequences of not being exit ready, both for the owner as well as for the business.

There is no doubt in my mind that every business owner wants to offer great products or services. We all want to solve a problem or fill a gap in the market, and I have yet to meet an owner who doesn't work hard and isn't passionate about what they do. Despite all of that, I am seeing time and time again owners:

- Who are not realising a return on investment for all the years of hard work and sacrifice.
- Who are retiring poor or having to pare back their standard of living.
- Who are forced to continue to work because they cannot afford to retire.
- Whose business, despite all their effort and years of hard work, is still not worth anything or not what they were hoping for.

A few years ago, I became increasingly frustrated at seeing numerous business owners who were either forced down a road that they did not want to go down or left with no options. Reflecting on my dealings with business owners looking to sell, I found three common causes that contributed to owners having the problems listed above, thus not having exit-ready businesses. These three common causes are:

- Perception
- Preparation
- Process

The Cause for Not Being Exit Ready: Perception

The first cause is the owner's lack of perception or understanding around exit planning. Over the years, I have found there to be six common misconceptions when it comes to selling a business relating to:

- Time
- Valuation
- Risk
- Transferable Value
- Deal Structure
- Business Brokers

Time

A common trend I see is owners planning their exits far too late. Many people do not realise that it ideally takes up to five years to prepare a business for sale. The question I often get asked is, 'Why will it take five years to prepare a business for sale?' There are two reasons for this five-year timescale:

1. Allowing five years gives the business owner a less intense process. It provides you time and space to consider options, make decisions and implement measures effectively, especially when it comes to preparing for the due diligence phase.

2. Buyers want to see trends. The five-year period will give buyers the opportunity to see how the business is performing. A buyer will want to see positive, sustainable trends which, if they can be seen, will add confidence and value to the business. As a buyer, what you do not want to see is a massive spike in sales or in profit just before the business goes to market, which is something I come across quite often. In these cases, the owner has either conducted a huge marketing exercise to increase sales or has implemented cost-saving

measures to increase profits. They tend to then use these increases in an attempt to justify their already overvalued company. The problem here is that no one knows if the increase in growth or cost saving is sustainable and realistic for the business. Buyers see right through this, so time, i.e., five years, allows the buyer to see what is really happening within the business and what is actually achievable.

Valuation

This is by far the biggest reason why deals collapse. Many business owners suffer from 'ugly baby syndrome', where the owner thinks their business is worth more than it actually is because they are emotionally attached to their business, which makes sense, considering they are its creator. I call this 'ugly baby syndrome' because when being honest about the state and value of an owner's business (their 'baby'), you receive the same reaction as you would if you told a mother her baby is ugly. To that mother, her baby is the most beautiful thing in the world, irrespective of its appearance! To a business owner, their business is precious and their investment of money, time, energy and effort can often cloud their judgement.

Valuations are incredibly emotive. The owner has poured their heart and soul into their business and dedicated years of toil and sacrifice. To that owner, their business is incredibly valuable because of the emotional tie they have to it. However, you cannot value a business on emotion, only on facts, and that is exactly what a buyer or investor will do.

Valuations are incredibly subjective. The value a buyer or investor places on a business will differ, depending on their individual needs, risk aversion, experience and desire to acquire. This means that, if you were to ask 100 people to value a business, you would probably get 100 different valuations! The key to a sensible and realistic valuation is to focus solely on the facts.

As you'll soon discover in part two of this book, there are several methods that can be used to calculate business value. Ideally, you should use at least three different methods to get a balanced average. One such method I have created is the Cash Flow Valuation method.

The Cash Flow Valuation method calculates what the business is worth based upon the cash flow it generates. This is really a sanity check, in much the same way that a bank checks your affordability for a loan or mortgage. It is a very quick and easy-to-use method, and it will give you a good idea of what your business is worth from a cash flow perspective.

Risk

The fact is that SMEs are riskier than larger businesses in excess of £2m EBITDA (earnings before interest, tax, depreciation and amortisation). These larger companies have the ability, resources, policies, procedures and manpower to grow and withstand the storms that come their way. Smaller businesses are somewhat limited in these areas, and it is these limitations that make SMEs riskier. Therefore, it is up to the owners of SMEs to reduce the risk as much as possible by implementing an exit strategy (the how-to of this we cover in part two). The owner can reduce a lot of the risk to a buyer by understanding where these risks lie and incorporating them using the most appropriate acquisition deal structure.

Transferable Value

The definition of transferable value is what a business is worth to a buyer without its previous owner, and it is determined by how well the business runs without that owner.

If the owner is solely responsible for generating a company's net profit or EBITDA, what happens when they leave the business? Would a buyer or investor be able to replicate or improve upon the results of the previous owner? In most cases, this outcome would be extremely unlikely, especially if there are no proper systems and processes in place.

Transferable value determines what happens after the owner leaves the business and dictates financial value for all SMEs. Because transferable value is not something you can touch and feel, it can be very difficult to measure and quantify. I've outlined a proven process that works in this book. We'll discuss how transferable value can be measured and tracked in later chapters, but for now, just know that transferable value tends to make up the majority of an SME's overall valuation.

Deal Structure

In my experience, this is the second biggest reason for the collapse of deals. Many owners do not understand deal structure, and because they do not understand it, when it is brought up during negotiations, they reject perfectly good offers. This lack of understanding may result in the owner thinking that the buyer is trying to cheat them or pull a fast one on them, or their expectations not being met in the way they were hoping.

Buyers and investors understand that there is always an element of risk when buying a business, so they use strategies to reduce those risks as much as possible. One of these strategies is to use deal structure.

However, problems arise when business owners hear of companies being bought out for millions of pounds or dollars because it causes them to believe that someone will simply knock on their office door ready to write them a huge cheque. This may happen to some SME owners, but it is incredibly rare. For the vast majority, there may be a small payment on completion (not always), and the rest will be funded over a period of time. Understanding the various possibilities when it comes to deal structure will create options for the owner, but these options will be heavily dependent upon how personally and financially prepared the owner is — all part of the 'three-legged stool' approach, which we'll discuss in a later chapter.

Addressing these key areas will give you an edge. It is a buyers' market, but by being prepared, you can use that to your advantage.

Business Brokers

Really good brokers work with businesses worth at least £2m to £5m or more. When you enter the mid to low market, especially with valuations less than £1m, you find brokers that are not so good. They give owners false hope by agreeing to represent their business. They do this because a) they do not know what makes a business saleable; and b) they don't know how to value a company (other than applying a three to five times multiple). Their main aim is to sign up as many businesses as possible, charging each seller a marketing fee of anything between £3k to £40k, and if they sell the business, well, that is just a bonus.

Business brokers won't admit to this but, on average, they only sell about 20% of the businesses they take on to their books.

Brokers use different methods to attract sellers and buyers alike. They are not bad in themselves; it is just how they go about their business that could be questionable.

Let's look at a few examples:

Seller Fees: This is where the seller pays for all the broker's fees, including marketing, and the broker takes a percentage of the sales price. This is a fairly old but standard way of selling a business.

Buyer Fees: This is becoming a slightly more popular method, where the seller pays nothing, but the buyer pays for everything. A great way to get many hundreds of sellers on the books, but the question remains: how many of these companies are actually saleable?

Hybrid: I've not seen many of these, but the seller pays an amount for marketing fees and the broker takes a small percentage of the sales price from both the seller and buyer.

All three options are perfectly legitimate methods that brokers use to sell businesses. What I have found, and continue to find, is that most brokers do not know how to value a business, nor do they ensure that the business is saleable in the first place. This means there are thousands of businesses currently on the market that will never sell, but the seller has still paid a fee for a broker to market their business or a buyer is paying a broker to find the right business for them to buy. Between these two arrangements, very little action is taking place.

At the end of the day, a broker's primary aim, goal and source of income is in signing up as many business owners (buyers or sellers) as possible. Many are not concerned with whether the business is ready for sale or even saleable.

The many brokers who charge the seller simply overpromise and convince the owner that they can sell their business for a massively overinflated, unsubstantiated valuation. This seduces the owner, and they end up signing a very arduous contract, normally tying them into a 12-to-24-month term. They proceed to charge the owner a ridiculous marketing fee to advertise on various websites, make a few phone calls and send out some emails. At this point, they consider their job done. If the business sells, that's a bonus.

Reasons for brokers' low success rates are that very few of them actually know how to value a business and many of them have never run a business themselves. Some are desperate to take on any business whose owner is willing to pay them a marketing fee.

This sector is unregulated and, in my opinion, in desperate need of change to bring confidence and integrity back into its marketspace.

I believe that the biggest opportunities await business owners who are prepared and have an exit strategy implemented. In doing so, they will avoid the common misconceptions and pitfalls of exit planning that cause a sale to collapse. When meeting with business owners, I see time and time again these six common misconceptions around selling a business. If these misconceptions can be addressed long before they need to exit, fewer deals will collapse. In part two, I will reveal the process for addressing all of these misconceptions.

The Cause for Not Being Exit Ready: Preparation

A lack of preparedness is the second reason so many business owners who are forced to exit do so in a terribly dissatisfying way. To understand the importance of preparation, we first need to address the realities of living in an unpredictable world and consider the possible events that a typical business owner may experience at some point in their life.

The reality is that every owner, irrespective of who they are and what their business does, must exit their business at some point. Their exit will be a result of one of the 7 Ds: deal, decide, distress, disagreement, disease/disability, divorce or death. Let's look at each 'D' and consider it in terms of preparation.

1. Deal

You may be contacted out of the blue by a potential buyer. Someone may approach you wanting to buy your business and, unbeknown to you, this may be the perfect time. However, if your business is not exit ready, you may not be in a position to attract the sort of valuation you were expecting. If, on the other hand, your business is exit ready, this could be just the opportunity you need to move on to the next chapter of your life. Preparation is key!

2. Decide

At some point along your journey, you may decide that this is the right time to exit. You feel you have achieved everything you set out to and now is the time to move on. If the business is exit ready, you'll know exactly what you're aiming for from the sale and this could increase the speed at which you can exit. On the other hand, if your business still needs to be prepared for exit, this will either delay your plans or reduce the value you were expecting to achieve. Either option could be very undesirable, depending on your personal circumstances.

3. Distress

You could find that you, on a personal level, or your business is going through a rough period. You may have reached the point where you no longer want to be in the business. You may no longer want the hassle, the stress, the struggle or the problems, and the only way out is for you to exit. At this point, you'll take whatever you can, and this will make you what is known as a 'motivated seller'. This is not necessarily a bad thing, provided you're willing to accept a possible reduction in valuation and be very flexible on deal structure. Depending on how flexible you're willing to be, you could exit quickly, but know that this will require compromise on your part.

4. Disagreement

This typically happens between shareholders or co-owners and can be an extremely complex and unpleasant situation in which to find yourself, especially if there have been no discussions or agreements as to what would happen should these circumstances arise. A comprehensive shareholders' agreement spells out what happens in these situations, saving much time, money and heartache. To avoid such upset and upheaval, ensure there is a detailed shareholders' agreement in place, or at least a memorandum of understanding.

5. Disease/Disability

Statistics show that around half of business owners will be forced to exit their business. Typically, this will be due to unexpected illness or disability of some form – a car accident, for example, the outcome of which could lead the owner to leave the business immediately or in the very near future. Alternatively, a change in personal circumstances may force an owner to exit, maybe through ill health, the death of a family member or some other event that will either force the owner to leave their business altogether or have their attention redirected away from the business for a period of time.

6. Divorce

This is a very unfortunate situation that I see some business owners having to face. Going through a divorce could impact the business, your motivation and your overall wealth-planning strategy. Divorce is a very difficult event to plan for – after all, who intentionally plans on getting divorced? The thing to be aware of here is, should this happen, it will inevitably impact you and/or the business on some level.

7. Death

The final 'D' is death, something from which none of us are exempt. Some people tell me they are never going to retire, that they plan on working until they die, which is fair enough, but death is not an exit strategy; death is an event. The issue here is that no one knows when that day will arrive. That's why we have insurance, a will and power of attorney in place to deal with matters, should it happen unexpectedly. The same goes for your business; an exit strategy looks at what will need to happen to your business in the event of your death. This will help make life much simpler and easier for your loved ones and your employees, preventing them from having to sort out a whole host of problems in your absence.

If a business is not in a perpetual state of exit readiness and attractiveness, when one of the above events happens, the business will either be unsaleable or it won't be ready for sale. This could cause its value to plummet and, if the owner is needing to exit very quickly due to a change in health or personal circumstances, it may lead to an unsuccessful exit.

We all know that life is unpredictable and there is nothing you can do to control it; the only thing you can do is prepare for all eventualities. That is why implementing an exit strategy is so important as it prepares the owner and the business for whatever the future holds. I believe every business needs to be exit ready as soon as possible for two reasons:

1. Should life throw you a curveball, you can respond in a controlled manner.

2. As the owner, you get to reap the rewards of having a business running as efficiently as possible in the interim, before you exit.

Being prepared gives the owner the very best chance of exiting the business successfully and realising a return for all their hard work.

Unfortunately, too many owners aren't getting prepared for this transition phase as can be seen in the following statistics (from EPI State of Owner Readiness Surveys and Business Optics Survey 2010–2019):

- 98% of business owners aren't adequately prepared for the due diligence phase, and this will not only increase the amount of time it will take to complete a deal, but will also cost considerably more.

- 88% have no exit team to help them prepare for and navigate through the exit process.
- 86% of owners are working hard and creating value in what they deliver to their customers, but when it comes time to sell, this value is not always transferable, causing the deal to collapse or the value to plummet.
- 83% have no written exit plan and even more have no post-exit plan, which is why getting the owner exit ready is just as important as getting the business exit ready.
- 81% do not know what their business is worth.
- Over 80% of an owner's net worth is tied up in their business.
- 76% do not have or are not familiar with all their exit options.
- 70% do not know the income they require to support their lifestyle post exit. They do not know 'Their Number'.
- 40% have no plans in place to cover a forced exit, such as those caused by illness, death, injury or divorce. The main effect of not being in a position to deal with such life events is that the owner's attention will get diverted elsewhere and the business suffers as a result. It is always worthwhile to plan for the unforeseen. Much like an insurance policy, you hope to never use it, but it is good to know it is there, just in case.

The Cause for Not Being Exit Ready: Process

The final reason behind so many owners not being exit ready and thus suffering unsuccessful exits is due to a lack of a process. Let me explain.

I am finding more and more owners who love what they do but find themselves getting bogged down in the mundane running of the business, where they firefight and sorting out problems, where they feel as if they take one step forward and then two steps back and where they struggle to gain any traction to move the business forward.

The Business By Design methodology provides a clear procedure to guide business owners through the exit planning process towards a clearly defined point of exit readiness. As with any strategic planning, this involves understanding your current position, knowing where you want to get to (your destination) and then planning a step-by-step route from A to B that gets you to your end goal – ready to exit within your planned timescale or ready to deal with any unexpected life events.

Understanding Your Current Position

Understanding your current position involves considering three key elements. You can think of these key elements as the three legs of a stool, where each need to be of equal strength and standing to bear the weight of the whole structure.

As a business owner, you have your business life, your personal life and your financial life. They are all separate, but they need to work symbiotically and be of equal priority and importance in order to create stability across your life as a whole.

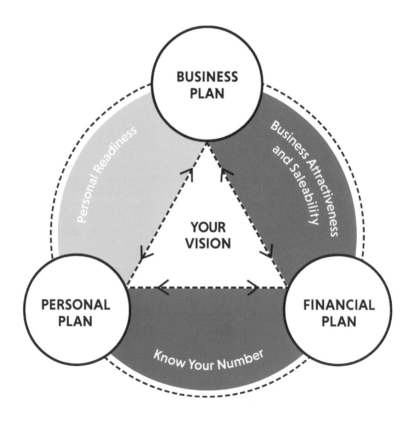

From a business perspective

For a start, many owners do not know what their business is worth. I have found that owners typically overvalue their business by at least 2.5 times its actual worth. They also do not have a clear understanding of how saleable their business is and what they need to do to reduce the risk profile and increase the overall value of the business.

From a personal perspective

Owners tend not to have a written plan for their own life post exit. Many invest a lot of their personal time and emotional energy into their business; as such, the business starts to become their identity. Exiting their business could lead to a lack of purpose and identity, which can have devastating consequences, such as getting divorced or making reckless financial decisions, which are not uncommon.

From a financial perspective

Many owners do not know what 'Their Number' is. This number is the amount of money needed in order to retire and live the lifestyle they want, without the fear of ever running out of money. Without knowing this number, they cannot determine how close or how far away they are from achieving their financial goals or freedom.

Understanding Your Destination

For the most part, owners have a general idea of where they want to go, but many do not know the exact details of where they need to be in terms of their destination.

Understanding the Route

More importantly, even if an owner does know where they are and where they want to get to, they usually don't know how to get there. They don't know the steps between their current position and their destination, nor do they have a process to help them reach their desired end point.

It is this lack of a clear process and strategy that causes many owners to lose their way or struggle to focus on the end goal: to exit successfully. Implementing the Business By Design methodology will give you that **Clarity** and **Control**, and by **Consistently** working on your Master Action Plan (MAP), you will get to your destination and **Complete** your journey. Part two of this book addresses each of these four phases of the process.

An exit strategy is all about knowing where you are and where you are going, then having a plan, a strategy, for how you will get there. The Business By Design methodology helps to create that clear focus and is incredibly strategic in ensuring all three legs of your stool – business, personal and financial plans – are equally prioritised and balanced.

Successful vs Unsuccessful Exits

As already discussed, every owner will have to exit their business at some point, whether it is by choice or by circumstance. As a business owner, it is within your control to determine whether that exit will be successful or unsuccessful, the result of which all hinges around your preparedness – whether or not you have an exit strategy in place well before your exit.

Unsuccessful Exits

There are two ways to unsuccessfully exit a business:
- Cannot sell
- Can sell

Unsuccessful Exit: Cannot Sell

This happens when the business is not ready for sale or is unsaleable. This leaves the owner with only two choices:

1. They are forced to close their business down.

2. If they were financially reliant on selling the business, they may need to continue working in the business until they have sufficient money to support their retirement plans.

Unsuccessful Exit: Can Sell

If the owner does manage to find a buyer to purchase their business, it is normally for a lot less than the owner was originally expecting or hoping for. This often results in a wealth gap (a discrepancy between the amount of money they have and the amount of money they need) that will need to be filled, making this situation far from ideal.

Successful Exits

For the minority of owners, there is the option of exiting their business successfully through one of the following ways:

- Using the business to fund their financial plan
- Planning liquidation
- Selling externally
- Selling internally
- Selling to family

We'll discuss the advantages and disadvantages of each of these options later on.

For now, business owners need to understand that this is a buyers' market. Here's how this can be used to your advantage as a business owner:

- By getting yourself exit ready and following the principles and ideas of the Business By Design methodology in this book, there is an opportunity to stand head and shoulders above the competition. Being exit ready will increase the speed of an acquisition, making it less expensive and thus more appealing to buyers.

- Start thinking like a buyer. Ask yourself, 'Would I really want to buy my business?' and be brutally honest with your reply. In everything you do, think about how your actions will benefit a potential buyer. Thinking in this way will benefit you both now and in the future, so it is a win-win!

- Start implementing an exit strategy as soon as possible to start maximising the return on your investment.

- Remember: An exit strategy is not a one-size-fits-all approach; the methodology for creating an exit strategy follows the process laid out in the next few chapters, but you will tailor the process to your own business and personal situation.

In the following chapters, we will look at the Stabilise-Systemise-Scale Process, part of the Business By Design methodology for getting your business exit ready. The first part of this process is to establish where you and your business are right now. With any journey, you have a starting point and a destination. There is absolutely no point in starting a journey without first understanding precisely where you are. Once we have established your starting point, we look to get a very clear vision of your destination – what you want your future to look like. Then, as you will discover, it is all about planning the journey and realising a return.

Chapter 2 Takeaways

- **There are three causes that contribute to a lack of exit planning:**
  - **Lack of perception**
  - **Lack of preparation**
  - **Lack of process**

- **By not being exit ready, business owners are leaving money on the table.**

- **You need to have a business, personal and financial plan and give equal priority and attention to each.**

- **You can choose to exit your business successfully or unsuccessfully.**

- **An exit plan, like any journey, involves understanding your starting position, knowing your destination and then planning a step-by-step route from A to B.**

CHAPTER 3

Simply Good Business (and Whole Life) Strategy

YET ANOTHER REASON to motivate you to create an exit strategy is that, in doing so, you must put into place good strategies – in your business and your whole life – so that you and your business run in a balanced and optimal manner. An exit strategy that you put in place today in order to exit your business years from now involves you establishing excellent practices that will support you and your business to run with balance and energy on a daily basis. In this way, an exit strategy is a two-for-one deal: you not only benefit when you finally exit, but you experience daily benefits as you journey towards your destination. Let's look at this in a bit more detail.

This chapter outlines how an exit plan considers all aspects of your life so that when you exit as well as in the interim, you are operating in all areas of your life with the greatest efficiency, satisfaction and balance.

The Three-Legged Stool

Let's revisit the concept of the three-legged stool that we briefly looked at in the previous chapter. As business owners, there are three key areas of our life:

- Business
- Personal
- Financial

Think of the principle of a three-legged stool or tripod: each leg needs to be of equal length and strength to bear equal weight so that the whole structure remains balanced and sturdy.

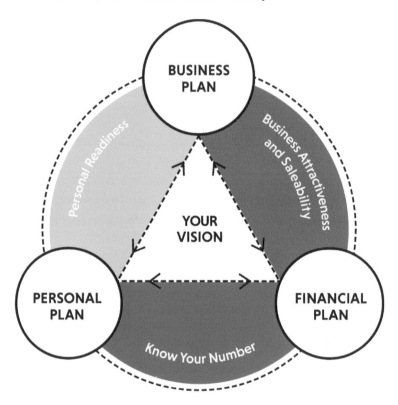

Looking back, I now realise that early on in my business career as I was growing and developing my businesses, when life felt out of control and at times overwhelming it was because one or two of my stool's legs were out of sync. Some areas were taking more priority than others; some were even pulling in a different direction altogether. As soon as there was an imbalance or misalignment, it led to stress in the whole structure.

Each of the three legs of the stool must have a common goal: they need to be aligned and working in synergy. Each area must be addressed in equal measure and carry the same importance. For most business owners, their main focus is on the business and little time or thought is placed on their personal life or their financial life. Although the impact of this may not be seen in the short term, as time moves on, the impact will begin to emerge. It is precisely when the owner wants to exit the business that the impact will be most prominent.

At times, throughout the various seasons of running a business, so many of us business owners (and I include myself here) find ourselves out of balance. From the very beginning, our business starts to create a life of its own, and we frequently find ourselves at the mercy of the 'monster' we have created.

At the end of a working day or period of time, do you find yourself wondering why you feel so exhausted? Or do you wonder how it is that you're working so hard, but it rarely feels as if you're actually getting anywhere or making progress? You've looked for ways to be more organised, more disciplined, you work longer hours, but the more you do, the more it feels like you're getting nowhere.

During the natural cycles of business growth, both you as the owner and the business itself need to change. With those changes come all sorts of challenges: hiring the right people; creating processes and systems to cope with the increase in demand; training, marketing, IT systems, human resources, legal policies, etc. If these aren't dealt with in a systematic and focused way, the business soon becomes overwhelming. The need to deal with all the issues at once leads the owner into a state of firefighting: doing just enough to keep the flames at bay but never putting the fire out completely. Just as one part of the fire dies down, another jumps back up, and so the vicious cycle continues – ever-busy but going nowhere fast. And all the while, the other two legs of your stool – the personal and financial parts of your life – remain neglected.

Creating an exit plan today – hopefully years or even decades before you want or need to exit – doesn't revolve around only making plans for your business. Because your whole life changes when you exit, the plan must involve all three main areas of your life – all three legs of the stool: your business, your personal life and your financial life. As such, creating an exit plan requires you to examine and address these three areas to check their current state and balance and then revisit them at regular intervals so that when you finally exit, you will have prepared yourself in a robust, balanced and holistic way.

The point of assessing and planning these three major parts of your life to create your exit plan is not only to benefit you when you finally do exit, but you should also notice immediate benefits to the way that your business runs and the rewards that you experience. In this way, making an exit plan isn't just something to help you later on; it enables you to scale your business and to create balance and fulfilment in all areas of your life during the time leading up to your exit, as well as afterwards. Put simply, it enables you to enjoy the journey as well as the destination. Let's look at these three legs of the stool individually so that you can get a glimpse of the kind of exploration you'll be doing when creating your exit plan.

The Business Leg of the Stool

In creating an exit plan for the future, you will assess your business in its present state in terms of its attractiveness, its saleability and its valuation. You will then revisit this assessment at regular quarterly and yearly intervals to reassess it and make necessary adjustments to realign it. These assessments will allow you to have the most successful exit possible whilst requiring you to put into place good business practices, which should lead to your business achieving its optimal growth potential.

Along with examining the business leg, you will also be looking at your personal and financial life so you can also enjoy a more balanced life overall. As I have stated, creating an exit strategy isn't simply a plan for your future; it's also a solid plan for bettering your life now. Let's look at those three parts of the business you'll be assessing when you create your exit plan: business attractiveness, business saleability and business valuation.

Business Attractiveness

No two businesses are the same; there are quirks, nuances and risks to every business. As such, we need to assess a business according to how it performs in its current condition, based upon its own merits. This involves assessing your business objectively from an outsider's point of view, in much the same way that a buyer or investor would.

In assessing a business's attractiveness, we look at the business's potential in its current condition and we assess it from a business, financial, market and investment point of view. This assessment is really to identify any key areas that need developing in order to make your business more attractive to a buyer for when the time comes to sell.

Business Saleability

Business saleability looks at the business from the inside for how saleable it is by examining the top ten value drivers to ascertain its level of exit readiness. These ten value drivers are:

- Customers and suppliers
- Dependency (internal)
- Exit readiness
- Financial data
- Growth potential
- Housekeeping
- Reputation
- Risk
- Shareholder alignment
- Systems and operations

Many owners of small- and medium-sized enterprises (SMEs) think that buyers or investors are only interested in the financials, the profit. This could not be further from the truth. Yes, the financials and profit are important, but there are many other factors that they will consider, all of which are important. Buyers and investors aren't looking to buy a problem or to purchase a job and, as such, will assess a business in several other areas to help them to evaluate its viability and value. As every business is different, every buyer is different, and they will have their own unique set of criteria and appetite for risk. However, as a business owner, you'll want to appeal to as wide of an audience as possible. As a result, by regularly addressing these value drivers as part of creating and then updating your exit plan, you'll stand a greater chance of selling your business when you want to do so. As you'll discover throughout this book, getting these value drivers ready is not a quick and easy task. Therefore, starting this process right from the beginning of a business, or at least as early as possible, will give you the best chance of a successful exit.

Business Valuation

Many people do not realise that when valuing a business, SMEs need to take into account both financial value *and* transferable value. If you have an EBITDA of more than £1m to £2m, you only really need to focus on the financial value as this indicates that all the systems and processes should already be in place. However, for any business with an EBITDA below £1m to £2m, transferable value plays a significant part in the overall valuation.

Financial value always follows transferable value. Let me use a barrel to demonstrate the point:

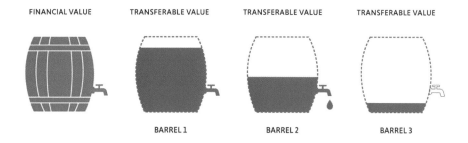

FINANCIAL VALUE   TRANSFERABLE VALUE   TRANSFERABLE VALUE   TRANSFERABLE VALUE

BARREL 1   BARREL 2   BARREL 3

The physical barrel represents the financial value of a business. The size and shape of the barrel is dictated by the financial results, the EBITDA, the tangible assets, the cash flow, etc. – that's what creates the actual barrel, the financial valuation.

But the majority of business owners don't realise the type of value they are using to *fill* the barrel and they sometimes forget that this value needs to remain in the barrel when they leave. This is the transferable value.

If the business is automated – there is a management team, risks are reduced, everything is in order – then the transferable value will be greater than or equal to the financial value. That is exactly what we want and what will make a business saleable, as can be seen in barrel 1.

However, if the business is owner dependent – there are no systems or processes in place and no one other than the owner knows how to run the business – the transferable value will leave when the owner leaves and the financial value will be dictated by how much transferable value is left, as can be seen in barrel 2.

There may come a point (and this does often happen) when so much of the transferable value has disappeared that the business becomes unsaleable, despite the fact that the actual barrel, the financial value, is still intact, as in barrel 3. This typically happens when the owner is responsible for most of the company's sales and profits, where they have built up, and are still in control of, the relationships with customers and suppliers.

Your Personal Life

Being a business owner demands a lot; the stakes are high. As the business grows, the demand for our time increases. If we aren't careful, we find ourselves working 10- to 15-hour days, returning home only to eat and sleep and then working or catching up on sleep during the weekend. Then, before we know it, the years have slipped away and we're left wondering where the time went. Our identity is wrapped tightly in our business, and we may pay very little attention to the other important parts of our lives. Living in this way impacts two main areas. The first is the outcome of the business sale, especially during the negotiation phase, and if (and this is a big 'if') the negotiations proceed successfully, the wider effects will most certainly be felt post exit.

The second area of impact is our emotional state.

Many business owners see their business as an extension of themselves, meaning they may have a skewed view of the business. If a buyer seems to criticise it, it is taken as a personal insult (remember the 'ugly baby' syndrome?). In this situation, emotions get in the way and the business owner is unable to see things clearly and objectively. This is one of the central reasons that deals collapse so early in the process: the owner is too emotionally attached to their business.

The other element that may affect us when transitioning from our business to another opportunity, which could include retirement, is post exit regret. At some point post exit, we may start to feel regret, failure and/or a lack of identity or purpose. These emotions will be more prominent if throughout the life of the business we failed to ensure that all other areas of our personal life were addressed rather than neglected.

Through the Business By Design methodology, in creating your exit plan you will look at 14 areas that affect your personal life:

- Achievement
- Business
- Character
- Emotional state
- Exit preparation
- Fun and recreation
- Health and fitness
- Intellectual development
- Life vision
- Love relationship
- Personal blocks
- Post-exit plans
- Quality of life
- Social life

When you create your exit strategy, you'll not only address the present state of your business, but you will also consider your personal life. In doing this, from the day you start creating your exit plan to the time you exit (hopefully) years later, you'll be regularly assessing and tweaking these key areas of your life to create balance and purpose. Exit planning allows you to live your best life now, as well as in the future when you do finally exit.

Your Financial Life

Consider the following question …

If you were to retire tomorrow and not work another day in your life until you die or reach the ripe old age of 100, how much money would you need in your bank account right now to fund the lifestyle you desire?

In other words, how much money would you need at retirement to live the lifestyle you hope for without the fear of ever running out of money?

Are you able to answer? Do you have any idea?

Very few people are able to answer that question, resulting in one of two outcomes:

1. Some business owners work for a lot longer than they need to. Because they don't assess how much money they will need to retire to live the life they want, they think they need more money than they actually do. Therefore, they end up working extra years in their business when in actual fact they already closed their wealth gap and could have retired years before.

2. Most business owners continue to work thinking that what they're doing is enough to achieve their retirement goals, but in the end, they realise it was not. By the time this realisation hits, it is too late and there is very little they can do to resolve it.

A vital part of preparing yourself for a successful exit is being crystal-clear as to your financial goals so that you can track whether you are on course. We will discuss this in more detail in part two.

Creating an exit plan today is a smart move for every aspect of your life. Not only will it prepare you for a successful exit from your business in the future, but addressing and reconciling the three main areas of your life – business, personal and financial – today will move you towards living a more balanced and satisfying life up until you exit, during the exit process and post exit. This is perhaps the strongest reason to create an exit plan for your business now rather than later; it's a gift that keeps on giving.

The next chapter presents yet another clear reason that will motivate you to create your exit plan now. In creating an exit plan, you'll be implementing systems to move your business from 'owner-centric' to 'value-centric', enabling you to act as CEO rather than 'head worker'. Being your company's CEO allows you to scale your business in the present as well as ensure its saleability in the future when you exit, whether by choice or not.

Chapter 3 Takeaways

- Exit planning looks at your business, your personal life and your financial life.

- Each aspect must be given equal priority and attention to achieve balance and stability.

- When looking at the business, we must assess its attractiveness, its saleability and its value.

- For SMEs, financial value is driven by transferable value.

- We must address our personal life outside of our business so that we can live a more fulfilling life whilst we continue working and be prepared for life post exit.

- We need to know 'Our Number' – the amount of money we will need at retirement – to know the financial goal we are working towards.

CHAPTER 4

From Owner Centric to Value Centric: Becoming a CEO

As a business owner, especially in the initial stages, you become chief cook and bottle washer. It is very easy to get distracted and consumed by the day-to-day tasks of running your business. In reality, this may not change. When first meeting clients, even those running businesses in the millions, I often find that they all face similar problems. They're trapped in the very centre of their business, making all the decisions, solving day-to-day problems and firefighting. Sometimes this happens through choice – an owner feels the need to control everything and refuses to let go – but often it is just the result of how the business has grown, where the owner hasn't had the time or the foresight to plan properly or implement robust systems or policies. Whatever the reason, the result is the same: the owner finds themselves trapped in the centre of their business, the confluence of all that happens, and the business is totally reliant and dependent upon them.

Over the years, I have found that business owners who remain central to their company's performance and success tend to have unsaleable businesses, or at very best their involvement reduces the company's valuation. This is because for a buyer, there is no guarantee that the business will be as successful without its current owner, which poses a major risk. Bill, the business owner whose story I gave in the introduction, is one such owner. As you've already read, Bill is in debt and desperate to sell but because his is an 'owner-centric' business, it is unfortunately unsaleable.

Creating an exit plan for your business today involves examining your business and, over time, implementing systems to ensure that you move it from being 'owner-centric' to being 'value-centric'. As the business owner, you move from being 'head worker' to being 'CEO', meaning you move from working *in* your business – fighting fires and doing other daily tasks – to working *on* your business, putting into place overarching systems and plans that add value to the business, which should not only ensure your business is saleable in the future, but also that it achieves a high valuation.

This is the focus of this chapter: how an 'owner-centric' business compares to a 'value-centric' business and how creating an exit plan will help you to implement the systems and practices required for you to move from acting as a head worker in an 'owner-centric' business to being CEO of a 'value-centric' business. At the end of the chapter, there is a test for you to take so that you can determine whether you are head worker or CEO of your business and therefore whether your business is owner- or value-centric. Do not be too concerned about the results. My aim in this chapter is to motivate you to start creating an exit plan for your business today; not because you are necessarily looking to exit your business any time soon but because it simply makes good business sense to have the plan in place.

Owner- vs Value-Centric Business

Let's start by looking at the two types of businesses: the 'owner-centric' business and the 'value-centric' business. An owner-centric or lifestyle business is one that generates a comfortable income for its owner, whose view and thinking is focused on the here and now, e.g., paying their bills, fulfilling orders, providing a service or producing a product. The business is viewed in terms of its sales and profits, with the owner acting as head worker in their business.

Obviously, when a business is first established, it will naturally be heavily dependent upon its owner. That's absolutely fine at the outset but, as time moves on, as the business grows, the dependency upon the owner as head worker needs to decrease. This will be done through the owner building a team around them who are willing and at times more able than the owner to take on the owner's knowledge, skills and expertise. This is the only way that a business can grow efficiently and be prepared for the eventual (or perhaps sudden) transfer when the owner exits.

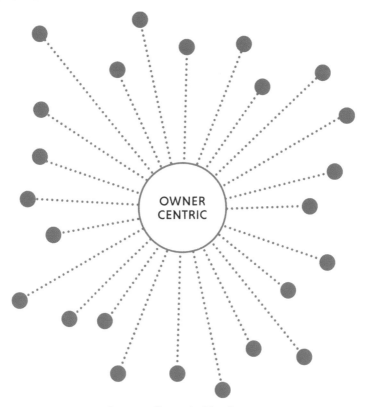

Owner-Centric Business

Every owner has a choice to make: either continue working *in* your business, staying as the expert and head worker and doing the things you find easy and comfortable, or choose to be the CEO of your company, a role that will allow you to work *on* your business. This role requires you to focus on three key areas within your business: finance, strategy and finding and nurturing talent. Those are the only three things on which a CEO should need to focus. You can employ and train people to take on day-to-day tasks. You need to understand that if you decide that it is easier to remain the expert in the business, focusing on the daily tasks and staying within your comfort zone, this will have a dramatic impact on the value and therefore the saleability of your business.

Let's now look at the value-centric business, whose model looks like this:

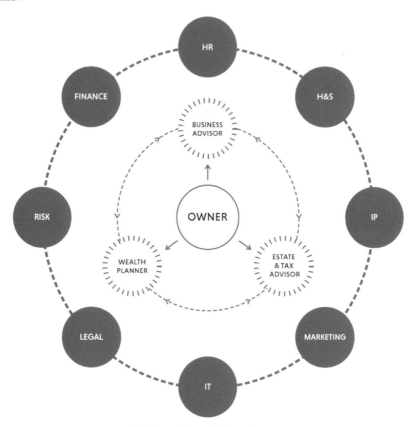

Value-Centric Business

In the diagram above, the owner is still central to the business, but there are fundamental differences when compared to the owner-centric model.

A value-centric business is a team game. Building a successful and valuable business will require the help and expertise of others. Owners who think they can operate on their own remain in the owner-centric model.

This is the critical difference: the owner of a value-centric business is surrounded by three key advisors: a wealth planner, an estate and tax planner and a business advisor. We will look at what each of these three advisors do for the CEO business owner so that you can better understand how implementing a value-centric business model for your business can set you up for a successful exit, as well as allow you to concentrate on growing your business rather than becoming caught up in the daily grind.

Wealth Planner

A wealth planner directs the process from a financial point of view. They take the information gathered from the business owner regarding their personal finances and, in conjunction with the tax and estate advisor, they create a personal wealth plan to help the owner achieve their desired financial goals before they retire or exit the business.

When beginning this planning process, there is typically a gap between the business owner's current position and where they want to be upon retirement. This is called the 'wealth gap'. The wealth planner's role is to identify and measure the gap, then implement strategies to help the business owner bridge the gap with a personal financial strategy.

My advice to all business owners out there is to not be reliant upon the sale or planned liquidation of their business to bridge their wealth gap. At the time of sale, the sector they are operating in may be in decline, there may not be many buyers out there or it could take a lot longer than expected. In the same way, if an owner is planning on liquidating the business, it may be that the assets within the business are not as valuable as previously thought or liquidating those assets may be more difficult. I would always recommend that the proceeds from the business, in whatever format it's in, is the cherry on the cake – it is the bonus on top of your personal wealth strategy. If you can achieve this, you will not be at the mercy of whatever economic situation is at play when you exit.

Knowing what your business is worth and exactly what your wealth gap is will put you in a position to make an informed decision as to when you can exit. Should you be approached by a potential buyer or undertake a planned liquidation to provide you with enough money to bridge your wealth gap, you will have a choice to make, but it will be an informed choice, which is key!

If, however, a large portion of the proceeds from the sale of the business is being used to bridge your wealth gap, your wealth planner will call on the expertise of a business advisor who will assess the current value of the business and what would be a realistic and achievable target value, given the timeframe they have to work within. The wealth planner then sets out to help bridge the wealth gap by implementing a personal investment plan.

Throughout the entire process, right up to the exit, both the wealth planner and business advisor work closely together to achieve the goals and ambitions of the business owner. (I encourage you to contact me and my team of accredited advisors at Business By Design to explore how we could support and advise you and your wealth planner.)

Estate and Tax Planner

The estate and tax planner looks at the findings that the wealth planner has gleaned from the business owner and considers the various ways to best structure the owner's estate and business affairs, with the aim of making it as robust and tax efficient as possible. They ensure the tax efficiency of both the owner's personal and business structure, makes use of every available benefit. It is worth having a proactive estate and tax planner on your team. We will explore this further in chapter 6.

Business Advisor

The business advisor is the linchpin in this system: the one that links all the parties together and works with the business owner to bring about those changes required by the wealth planner and estate and tax planner. Taking the information from the wealth planner and estate and tax planner, they work with the owner to develop the business so that it can be used to bridge the wealth gap.

The business advisor acts as the 'field general', working with the business owner, the wealth planner and the estate and tax planner to ensure there is always clear communication between parties and a coordination of the business strategy that ties in with the business owner's personal wealth strategy. They are the person who draws everything together and keeps things on track.

The business advisor undertakes all things business-related and is responsible for assisting the owner with growing their business in such a way to create value that can be transferred when the owner exits.

For the business owner, having an advocate acting on their behalf to ensure that the long-term strategies are in play allows them to focus on growing and adding value to the business.

Any good and experienced business advisor will have a team of experts around them – trusted people they can call upon to advise on a certain matter, to work on a particular aspect or to solve a problem. I refer to this group of experts as the special advisory service (SAS). Much like the military SAS, these experts are parachuted in to carry out a specific task as quickly and efficiently as possible and then they get out. They do not stay in the business for a sustained period of time, nor do they need to. This allows the owner to continue to focus on the business, leaving a particular situation to be dealt with by people who are proficient and experienced with that issue.

To ensure the business owner always gets the best and most effective assistance, the business advisor will have a full team of experts behind them that they can call on to work on specific tasks and particular issues.

It is imperative that every business owner building a value-centric business has these three people working alongside them. No one is an expert in everything, so having people to call on for specific expertise greatly benefits business development. Plus, having regular contact with people who aren't directly involved in the business offers a fresh perspective, leading to valuable objective insights that can be acted upon most effectively.

The Test

Having read the descriptions of owner-centric and value-centric businesses, hopefully, you now realise the benefits of putting into place today an exit strategy that will shape your business to be value centric with you as CEO rather than owner centric with you as head worker. I hope you understand how greatly you'll benefit when you exit (whether it is forced or planned) as well as in the interim. Now it's time for you to take a test to determine exactly how dependent your business is on you.

Owner-Dependency Test

How do you determine where you sit on the owner-dependency scale and how do you assess your performance as your company's CEO? Take the holiday test.

What do you think would happen to your business if you were to take a three- to six-month holiday? That means your laptop and your mobile phone are left on your office desk, you're effectively off the grid and no one can contact you.

Would you return to find your business has grown? Would it have managed to maintain its current performance? Or would you have lost business and returned to chaos? It's a scary thought for some, but it is a true test of how reliant your business is upon you being present and contactable, day in, day out.

CEO Test

As mentioned earlier, the role of a company's CEO is to focus on three core elements: finance, strategy and finding and nurturing talent. To find out how you're performing as the CEO of your business, take an inventory of your time over the next four weeks.

Create four columns with the following headings: *finance, strategy, talent and stuff* similar to this table:

Finance	Strategy	Talent	Stuff

Over the course of the four weeks, document how much time you spend on tasks and activities related to each column. At the end of the four weeks, calculate how much time you spent working in each area.

From personal experience with my own businesses and the clients with whom I work, I suspect that the column that has accrued the most items and greatest amount of time will be the 'Stuff' column.

Stuff
Answering all incoming phone calls
Completing all staff timesheets
Undertaking payroll each month
Doing the weekly bookkeeping
Ensuring all information is backed up and secure
Ensuring the office is clean, including the kitchen

Once you have a clear overview of how your time is spent, take all the tasks listed under the 'Stuff' column and group them into similar functions or areas of responsibility.

Stuff
A: Answering all incoming phone calls
A: Ensuring the office is clean, including the kitchen
B: Completing all staff timesheets
B: Undertaking payroll each month
B: Doing the weekly bookkeeping
C: Ensuring all information is backed up and secure

By grouping tasks together, you'll be able to see which jobs could be delegated to current staff members. If some tasks cannot be delegated to others, look to see if those tasks can either be bought into the company or farmed out to an organisation, such as a virtual assistant, IT contractor or HR consultant.

If you're a very small company, this may not be possible right now, but by starting to group tasks together in this way, you'll be starting to create a job description for your next member of staff or setting up the prospect of some tasks being contracted out to external companies. The idea here is to look for areas that are taking up your time but could be delegated to someone else, thus freeing up your capacity and allowing you to focus on the more important and specific tasks of running your business.

I appreciate that making these changes to how you and your staff work is easier said than done, but the key is to raise your awareness. Start by taking stock of what is taking up most of your time and then delegate it to your employees or an outside party. Train up or employ people to take those tasks off your hands. You will then be able to carve out time to be your company's CEO, focusing on your company's strategy, talent acquisition and finances.

As the owner of your business and the only person who can gain control of your business and personal future, I cannot urge you strongly enough: start creating your exit plan today. In creating an exit plan, you'll put strategies into place that move you from being head worker in your owner-dependent business to being CEO of your value-centric business. Doing that will not only improve your work-life balance while you still have the business, but you'll also start to create a more saleable business for when the time comes to pass it on.

Chapter 4 Takeaways

- A business that is reliant on its owner being present and handling day-to-day tasks and issues is dependent on its owner and is therefore owner centric.

- A business that can run independently of its owner on a day-to-day basis, with staff or external organisations carrying out most tasks and processes, is value centric.

- An owner-centric business will have less transferable value than a value-centric business.

- In a value-centric business, the owner acts as its CEO, focusing on finance, strategy and finding and nurturing talent.

- As CEO of a value-centric business, the owner will use the expertise and guidance of a wealth planner, a tax and estate planner and a business advisor.

- You can take the holiday test to find out how dependent your business is on you.

- You can take an owner-dependency test to evaluate how and where you spend your time and to start to plan how you will transition from head worker in your business to CEO of your business.

- Even if your business is small and you are in the early stages, you can start to plan for how you will transition from head worker to CEO in the future.

Congratulations! You've stuck with me through part one! My hope is that through reading this first part of the book, you have gained a clear idea of what exit planning is and why it is so important to start exit planning as early as possible in your business journey. (I have been quite emphatic about this!) You should now understand the difference between an owner-centric and value-centric business and how this difference affects the transferable value, and therefore the overall value, of your business. I will introduce you to the Business By Design methodology in part two, where we ascertain our current starting point in our business, personal life and financial life; set goals for where we would like to be in these three areas upon exiting our business; and plan a step-by-step route from A to B. I will take each stage of the process – from the initial assessments and valuations to enjoying a life post exit – and explain the principles behind each phase. I set out practical steps to guide you through the methodology for creating your exit plan, not only for the time when you exit, but also to bring balance and order to your business and your life in the interim so that you are ready to tackle whatever life may bring. As already stated, exit planning is simply good business strategy, so you will benefit in the here and now as well as in the future.

So, join me for part two, where we navigate together through the Business By Design methodology that will support you on your exit-planning journey.

PART TWO

The Methodology

THE SECOND PART of this book delves deeper into the methodology of exit planning: the raw ingredients that go into creating and implementing an exit strategy. These steps allow you to gain **Clarity**, increase **Control** and establish **Consistency** to finally **Complete** your goal – to exit successfully – whether you are ready to make that exit or if it is forced upon you unexpectedly due to unforeseen life circumstances. This process is extremely focused and strategic; it is designed to get you from where you are now, wherever that may be, to the place of exit readiness. It takes into consideration the three legs of the stool (the three key elements required to make this happen): a business plan, a personal plan and a financial plan. An essential element of this process is demonstrating how to move from an owner-centric business model to a value-centric business model.

By following the Business By Design methodology through this book, you'll feel confident to take the next steps in preparing your business for exit and to prepare yourself for whatever life may throw at you.

Before moving into the details, let's first take an overview of the Business by Design methodology.

The Business By Design Methodology In Action:

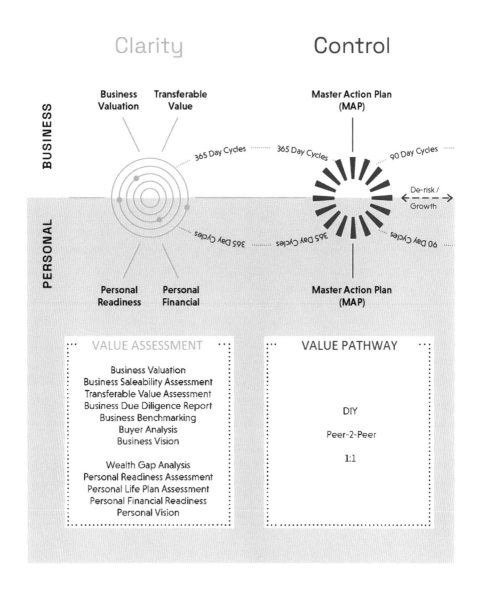

Consistency

Completion

Business
Review

Successful
Exit

BUSINESS

90 Day Cycles

De-risk /
Growth

90 Day Cycles

PERSONAL

Personal
Review

New
Beginnings

```
·····                          ·····          ·····                          ·····
:  VALUE CREATION    ·  :          :·  VALUE REALISATION     ·  :

  Surrounded by a Team of Experts
  Increased Transferable Value
  Increased Financial Value
  Reduced Owner Reliance
                                                   More Options
  Work-Life Balance                                Successful Exit

  Know Your Number
  Personally Prepared
  7 D Preparation Plan
  Personal Investment Strategy
·····                          ·····          ·····                          ·····
```

The Business By Design Phases:

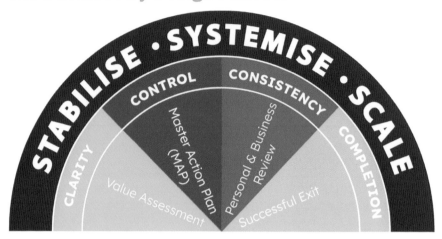

The Stabilise-Systemise-Scale Process is a holistic approach to exit planning. It consists of four key phases:

- Clarity
- Control
- Consistency
- Completion

Clarity

In order to gain Clarity, you need to know and understand three important components:

1. **Current situation (location):** You need to assess three aspects: how your business is currently performing; where you are personally, both as a business owner and as an individual; and your current financial position.

2. **Your vision (destination):** It is vital to know where you want to go. You need to understand the vision for your business, your plans for life post business and how much money you will need to be able to live the lifestyle you want.

3. **The pathway:** Once you know your current location and your ultimate destination, you need to find the best path to enable you to move from where you are now to your destination.

We extract this information using the Value Assessment Tool, which allows you to get a very clear picture of where you are now and where you want to be in the future. Once we know your location and your destination, we are then able to plot a course to help move you from where you are now to where you need to be using a MAP (Master Action Plan). Created using the Value Assessment, a Master Action Plan is a list of all the areas that need to be addressed within your business, your personal life and your finances to help get you to your destination. Ideally, a Value Assessment should be carried out annually to gauge and measure your progress over the last 12 months, update your future plans if they have changed and determine which areas need work in the coming 12 months.

Control

Once you have gained Clarity, you are in Control, meaning that you control your business rather than your business controlling you. At this point, you will have your MAP (Master Action Plan) that provides you with a list of all the areas that need to be developed or tasks that need to be completed to get you to your destination. Think of this list as a set of waypoints to help guide you step-by-step to your end goal. You choose a number of tasks to work on within your business and tasks to work on personally which are then reviewed after 90 days. I would suggest no more than five tasks to work on within your business and five personal and financial tasks (ten tasks in total) per 90-day cycle.

As every owner is unique with varying degrees of experience, differing levels of network contacts and variable timescales available to them, how you navigate this part of the journey (called the Value Pathway) is flexible; you can choose which of the three routes will work best for you.

1. **Do-It-Yourself (DIY):** At this stage, you have all the information you need to get you to your destination. All you have to
   do is work on the MAP, focusing on your de-risking and
   growth activities, all of which will be highlighted in your
   Master Action Plan.

2. **Join a Peer-to-Peer Group:** Some business owners prefer to
   undertake this journey with other like-minded entrepreneurs.

There is security in being part of a group of people under-taking the same journey. There is strength in numbers, and if one owner is struggling, the resources and input of the group can help them to move forward.

3. **One-to-One:** For those owners who would like to take a more accelerated approach, there is a one-to-one option. Whilst an intense experience, you will cover a lot more ground, using the team and resources of a Business By Design approved advisor.

At Business By Design, our team of approved advisors and other experts would be delighted to partner with you to support you on your journey, whether 1:1 or part of a group. If either of these is your preferred route, contact us at **hello@businessbydesign.co.uk** to find out more.

Consistency

Once you have gained control, it's all about establishing consistency. Now you are clear on where you are and where you want to go, and you have your MAP (Master Action Plan) of how to get there. From here it is all about consistently working on your business and personal/financial tasks and constantly reviewing those tasks every 90 days. At each 90-day checkpoint, you will review which tasks have been completed and which are ongoing. You then refer back to your MAP to choose another set of tasks – again, choosing no more than five business and five personal/financial tasks per 90-day cycle. By consistently working on your business and working steadily through the tasks on your MAP, you will begin to make progress within your three plans and start to create real value in your business.

Whilst working through this process, you will start to create a team around you – your very own team of experts that can be called upon when needed. In doing so, your business will become less reliant upon you, which not only means that you will gradually be released from the day-to-day running of the business, but also that the business will increase in both financial and transferable value. You will start to achieve a better work-life balance and you will begin to prepare yourself for your post-exit life. You will also become prepared for any curveballs that life may throw you along the way. From a financial perspective, you will know Your Number – the amount of money you will need at retirement in order to live the lifestyle you want – and you will be creating a personal investment strategy to help make that a reality.

Completion

The final phase of the process is to complete a successful exit from your business and realise the value that you have created, which will allow you to move on to new beginnings, whatever they may be. This is only made possible by consistently working on your MAP (Master Action Plan) every 90 days and by carrying out a Value Assessment every 12 months to review the progress made to your business, personal and financial plans

The process of moving a business from an 'owner-centric' model to a 'value-centric' model is extremely focused and strategic. As discussed in part one of this book, every owner, irrespective of the type of business, will have to exit their business at some point. So, in order that your certain exit is successful, my aim is to provide you with the knowledge and tools to give you the best chance of creating, implementing and executing a considered exit strategy, rather than leave it to chance.

To undertake a free mini Value Assessment and receive a free mini MAP (Master Action Plan) please visit: **www.thesmarterexit.com**

Now that you have an overview of the Business By Design methodology in its four phases, let's turn to details, starting with Phase 1: Clarity.

Part Two – The Methodology Takeaways

- The Business By Design methodology consists of four phases: Clarity, Control, Consistency and Completion.

- To gain Clarity about your business, personal life and finances, you need to understand where you are now (your current situation), where you want to get to (your vision or destination) and how to create a pathway to get you to where you want to be.

- Once Clarity is gained, a plan can be drawn up to move your business, personal life and finances from their current state towards your destination.

- You have options for how you can work on your plan: DIY, as part of a group or 1:1 with a Business By Design advisor.

- You work on your plan in 90-day cycles, enabling you to build consistency into the way your business, personal life and finances develop.

- Finally, you reach the Completion phase, exiting your business successfully and realising the value you have created throughout the process.

CHAPTER 5

Value Assessment

IN PART ONE, you learned *why* it is crucial that you start getting your business exit ready. In part two, you will learn *how* to do so. It shouldn't be surprising that becoming exit ready is not a one-off task as you, your business and your finances are ever-growing and evolving. Getting exit ready entails revisiting your plans, goals and milestones at regular intervals, hence the 90-day cycle. However, as you'll soon learn, when creating an exit plan, the majority of the effort happens at the front end.

Current Location and Future Destination

If I dropped you off at a random place on planet Earth, gave you a map and compass and asked you to make your way to a certain tiny village in France, what would you do?

To have any hope of reaching your destination, you would first need to learn three things:

1. Where you are on the map – your current location
2. The location of the village in France – your destination
3. What the best routes between your current location and destination are

Once you establish these two points and have mapped out a route to your target destination, you must then follow the map you have created. As you move along your journey, you'll need to stop at regular intervals to recheck your location, assess how the progress you've made aligns with your ultimate destination and make adjustments as you see fit.

Of course, different people will opt for different routes, modes of transport and waypoints, but in the end, everyone should find their way to that tiny village in France.

The exact same principle works for exit planning. In this chapter, we're first going to get Clarity on: 1) your current location in terms of your business, personal and financial life (remember those three legs of the stool?), and 2) your destination (where you aim to be in those three parts of your life when you exit your business). By understanding these two points, we'll be able to create a tailored Master Action Plan (MAP) to help get you from where you are now to where you want to be. You can expect to review your progress at regular intervals to assess how it lines up with your destination and make slight changes as needed to keep you on course.

Clarity: Is It a Goat or Is It a Bird?

After reading part one, I hope you're already well versed in the dangers, denials and disappointments that are highly likely to be at play for a business owner who tries to exit a business without a plan in place. As I shared in the introduction, Bill's and Sarah's attempted exits were either impossible or far from ideal for a number of reasons – chiefly, both owners' lack of Clarity. Both were convinced that their businesses would be a precious jewel, coveted by any buyer. However, to prospective buyers, their businesses appeared to be of little to no value. What was going on? Quite simply, in both instances, the business owner and prospective buyers were looking at the same thing but from different perspectives.

In the image that follows, what do you see – a goat or a bird?

This is a classic example of how two people could be *looking* at the same thing with one *seeing* something completely different than the other. This same lack of Clarity applies to the buying and selling of businesses.

Overcoming Ugly Baby Syndrome

Whilst a business owner might see the business they are trying to sell as a wonderful opportunity, a buyer might very well only see its risks, view it as a job, and uncover a whole host of problems. A buyer would then take this into account when valuing the business. When these differing views collide, it causes conflict and emotions to run high. I call this phenomenon 'ugly baby syndrome'. We already talked about this phenomenon in part one, but let's revisit it here briefly.

I'm sure there are many of you who have seen a baby and thought to yourself, 'That poor thing is one ugly-looking baby', regardless of what the parents of that baby feel. For every parent, their baby is the most beautiful thing in the world. It does not matter what you or I think; to the parents who have carried the baby in the womb for nine months, thought about it every day, prepared for its arrival, painfully endured the birth and now finally have the baby nursing in their arms, it is a precious and beautiful baby. This is the fruit of them – all their dreams, desires and aspirations.

What sort of reaction would you expect to receive if you walked up to those parents and informed them that their baby was actually one of the ugliest babies you've ever seen? You may be perfectly correct; it could be the ugliest baby you've ever seen. Your claim could even be backed up by scientific proof and market research. There is nothing wrong with your assessment of how ugly this baby really is; however, if you did that, (from a health and safety perspective, I advise you never to do this!) the reaction you would receive would be a vicious attack from the parents defending their baby.

When it comes to a buyer valuing a business, in essence, this is exactly what they're doing. They're telling the business owner – who has invested their heart, soul, blood, sweat, tears and time into something that has been a constant companion throughout their life, that has seen their children grow up, that has provided everything they needed – you get the idea – that their business is not worth what they believe it is. In fact, on so many occasions, I have had to tell an owner that their business is not worth anywhere near their expected valuation, and the reaction I get each time is the reaction I would expect to receive if I had told a parent that their baby is ugly.

Let me give you an example of a business owner I met who was looking to sell his business so that he could retire.

The business was an estate agency that the owner had started 27 years ago. He'd built up a good brand name and was well known and trusted within the community. The business saw his children through schooling, paid for the family home, bought the office from which the business was trading, allowed the family nice holidays, etc. It was a business that had served the owner very well. Sadly, the owner was hit by one of the 7 Ds – death. Tragically, his wife became ill, and after a long period of illness, she passed away. Naturally, this took a huge toll on him, and during her illness and subsequent death, his attention was diverted away from his business. Unfortunately, his business partner, a minority shareholder, was not up to the job of running the business, and he allowed the business to deteriorate whilst the owner focused on his family. At the time we met, the main owner had been back in the driving seat for a few years and he was also in a new relationship. His realisation that life is fragile and that he was not getting any younger spurred him to put his business up for sale. His dream was to spend his remaining time enjoying life with his new partner, his children and his grandchildren.

The business was slowly recovering from the period of mis-management, incompetence and increase in local competition whilst the owner had been dealing with his personal tragedy. He was on target for £8,000 in net profit that financial year – the first time in four years that he was due to make a profit. The business was in debt of around £180,000, and the balance sheet was negative.

Initially, I hadn't been aware of how his business was performing financially as he was only prepared to share these details with me face to face. As I had several other meetings scheduled near to his office location, we agreed to meet for a coffee.

So that you can see how this plays out in so many instances of buyer/seller perceptions, I shall share with you our contrasting perspectives in the two tables below.

Business owner's perspective:

The business was a well-established name and brand.	✓
The business had been trading for over 27 years.	✓
The business provided a good living and opportunities for him and his family.	✓
A significant amount of blood, sweat and tears were invested into the business.	✓
Selling the business would have been instrumental in funding his retirement and provided the opportunity to travel.	✓
He had loyal members of staff who had been with him for many years.	✓
He enjoyed closing the sales and being well liked within the community.	✓
The expectation was to walk away on completion with a large cheque from a buyer.	✓
The business had gone through a rough patch, but the prospects were amazing for the right buyer to take it to the 'next level', especially if they improved the marketing.	✓
If the buyer were able to set up a letting side of the business, it would increase the potential even further.	✓

Buyer's perspective:

Well-established name and brand.	✓
The name and brand happened to be the owner's name – which posed a risk, especially in the location he was in.	✗
The owner was well known and respected within the community, the driving force behind the success of the business.	✗
I happened to know that the local area in which he was operating was notoriously difficult to penetrate due to people's loyalty to well-established brands, especially for this sector.	✗
The owner was still involved in the day-to-day running of the business and instrumental in most of the sales.	✗
Two of the key staff members were also around retirement age.	✗
As the owner was the landlord of the business premises, the rental charge was less than market value, but this would increase in line with market rates once he sold the business.	✗
There was no branch manager who could take over the day-to-day running of the business.	✗
The business only had a sales side and no letting side, resulting in an imbalance within the business model.	✗
The balance sheet was negative, with the debt being personally guaranteed by the owner.	✗

The value the owner placed on the business was £500,000. When asked to explain how he got to this valuation, he said that he still owed £180,000, which he would have to settle on completion. This would leave him £320,000, and after 27 years of hard work, the business had to be worth at least that. This amount would allow him to live the life he wanted when he retired. So to him, £500,000 was a fair price for what he believed the business to be worth. (Remember the ugly baby syndrome? We have one right here.)

As you'll find out later when we look at how to value a business based upon its financials, you'll clearly see that it was impossible to reconcile an £8,000 profit to a £500,000 valuation – an eye-watering multiple of 62 x EBITDA using that valuation method!

The owner thought it fair and reasonable that I should pay off his debts and provide him with the lifestyle he wanted in return for a business that would ultimately create a huge loss when the rent increased and a branch manager was put in place.

When assessing this business, other concerns that were going through my mind included:

- Having to hire a branch manager would cost around £50,000 plus bonuses
- The current owner owned the building which housed the business office, so the rent would increase from £5,000 to approximately £16,000 per year in line with market rates.
- Hiring and training new staff to replace the staff members nearing retirement age would incur more costs and time investment.
- The reaction of the local community once they knew the owner had left the business would likely be an issue.
- The need to increase and improve marketing to reclaim some of the market share lost to competitors over the years
- A letting arm would need to be set up to smooth the lumpy cash flow.
- The need for a return on my investment
- The need to pay for the actual sale of the business

As you can see, the £8,000 profit the business was due to make would not go far. In fact, the losses and risks associated with this business did not make this a viable opportunity, even if the owner gave the business away for free and simply walked away.

No matter how I tried to explain this, the owner only saw the upside, the future potential, and was not interested in or did not want to understand what I was explaining to him. He could not grasp the fact that in its current condition, his business was not a viable option for any buyer. He simply could not see the risks or problems that a new owner would have to face. In the end, I had to bring the meeting to a close as this was not an opportunity worth pursuing.

This business needed at least another five years, not only to be financially ready, but also to put the various systems and procedures in place and allow the owner to demonstrate the full potential that the business had to offer. The problem here was that the owner did not want to invest time and energy for another five years. In other words, he was too late in getting his business exit ready.

To avoid having ugly baby syndrome, the solution is to detach yourself emotionally from the business and look at it with Clarity from a buyer's perspective. With this clear and objective perspective, you can start to make decisions about your business with the end in mind, and through the eyes of a potential buyer. Doing this will ensure a laser-like focus, and anything you do within the business will be viewed from that perspective, which will ultimately affect the final outcome of ensuring you exit your business successfully.

Gaining Clarity about your current location and your ultimate destination is the first stage of getting exit ready. You obtain that Clarity through undertaking the Value Assessment for all three parts of your life – the three legs of the stool, as first mentioned in part one – the business, personal and financial plans for your life in terms of where you are currently (your current location) and your vision for the future (your destination).

The Value Assessment

The Value Assessment offers a holistic approach to assess the three key elements that will define you and your business to bring you Clarity in these three areas. These key elements are constantly changing, which is why it is advisable to revisit this assessment every 12 months. The Value Assessment acts as a marker that allows you to establish how far you have progressed and determine whether you're still on track, depending on any changes during the past year. It also allows you to readjust and refocus your business, personal and financial plans for the next 12 months. The key areas of the Value Assessment include the following:

- **Your Business Plan**
  - Business attractiveness assessment
  - Business saleability assessment
  - Business valuation (transferable and financial valuations)
  - Business financial due diligence and benchmarking
  - Buyer and exit analysis

- **Your Personal Plan**
  - Personal readiness assessment

- **Your Financial Plan**
  - Personal financial readiness
  - Wealth gap analysis

As in the three-legged stool example, it is about keeping everything in balance. If we take a top-level view of the three-legged stool, this is what the Value Assessment will assess:

With your vision as the focus, you create a business plan, a personal plan and a financial plan to achieve your goals and objectives. These plans are based upon your current position for each of your three aspects at the time of undertaking the Value Assessment. This forms part of the Stabilise-Systemise-Scale Process, where you take time out each year to assess your current location along your journey and create a reference point, using your Master Action Plan (MAP) as your guide. You can then determine which tasks and objectives need to be set in each of your three plans for the next 12 months to move you closer to your destination, your vision. In the shorter term, progress towards these chosen tasks and objectives is reviewed every 90 days throughout the year. This ensures focus and creates a rhythm, a culture, within the business that promotes continuous improvement, development and review. This is what I alluded to in part one when I showed you that getting exit ready doesn't only benefit you upon your exit but also in the interim, optimally scaling and developing your business (as well as the personal and financial parts of your life) throughout all the years leading up to your exit.

Here, you have choices: you may decide to pursue getting your business exit ready alone, opt to be part of a group of like-minded entrepreneurs or choose to work 1:1 with an approved Business By Design advisor. These options mean that you can choose the route best suited to you. You may feel well equipped to go it alone; however, working as part of a group or working 1:1 with an approved Business By Design advisor will provide you with access to a team of people who will hold you accountable and share their resources and many years of experience with you, not only to improve your chances of success, but also to help you to reach your goals more quickly.

In the following chapter, we will delve a little deeper. Using the Value Assessment, we will look at the first element of the Clarity phase: your business plan.

Chapter 5 Takeaways

- The same business can be perceived in different ways by the owner and potential buyer.

- Differing views of a business can lead to a discrepancy in valuations.

- To avoid such discrepancies, you need to gain Clarity and view your business from a buyer's perspective.

- Each of these three aspects – business, personal and financial – must be in balance (the three-legged stool) to achieve a stable foundation for your exit plan.

CHAPTER 6

Your Business Plan

To GAIN CLARITY about the current position of your business, your personal life and your finances, do a Value Assessment for each. I call the Value Assessment of the business 'the business plan', and it consists of five main elements:

- Business attractiveness assessment: looking at your business from the outside
- Business saleability assessment: looking at your business from the inside
- Business valuation: transferable and financial valuations
- Business financial due diligence and benchmarking: business financial performance
- Buyer and exit analysis: ascertaining the best exit for you

In this chapter, we look at these five elements of the business plan for your Value Assessment.

Elements 1 and 2: Business Attractiveness vs Saleability

Attractiveness and saleability are completely different elements of a business. In my own search for acquisitions, I have found some companies to be very attractive from the outside, but after looking at how the business is run from the inside, I find the business to not be ready for sale and, in most cases, unsaleable.

To give you an example, let's suppose you are buying or renting a property, as I am sure most of us have experienced this at some point. You browse through the online listings and find a property that meets all your needs. From the photographs and description, it looks to be the perfect property and in great condition, so you arrange a viewing. However, once inside the house, you find cracks in the walls, rising damp, and the property is in need of significant repairs. You are instantly disappointed because the impression you had been given of the property was not the same in reality. You get that all-too-familiar feeling in the pit of your stomach that this property is not right for you. So, what has happened to cause this?

From the outside – the photographs and description – the property looked very attractive. It was all in the way the photographs were taken and what was said in the description that sold it for you. There is no doubt the property looked attractive! However, it was only when you had a closer look and viewed the property from the inside that you realised the property was not as attractive as you previously thought. In other words, the property was not ready for sale or for rent. The owner still had a lot of work to do to bring the property up to the standard that you were initially expecting based on how the property was portrayed in the online listing. In this situation, the owner has a few options: a) take the property off the market and spend time addressing the necessary repairs before re-marketing, b) keep the property on the market at the same price and wait in the hope that a buyer or tenant is blinded by the outward attractiveness of the property and doesn't have the knowledge to investigate the inside too closely, c) accept a hugely reduced offer that reflects that amount of work required to bring the property up to standard, or d) admit defeat and withdraw the property from the market altogether.

The same applies to your business. It needs to be attractive from the outside as well as ready and saleable on the inside, and all this well before being put on the market. Most owners will put their best foot forward and show their business in the best possible light (attractiveness), but as soon as the seller starts the basic due diligence process (akin to an internal viewing and professional survey on a property), the business does not meet their expectations of saleability. This will be reflected in a greatly reduced valuation or in the deal collapsing altogether. Therefore, business *saleability* is just as important as business *attractiveness* – they go hand in hand – and to achieve a successful exit, the inside must be at the same standard as the outside.

Element 1—Business Attractiveness Assessment

Continuing with the house sale analogy, business attractiveness is like having the outside of your house in the best possible condition. Business attractiveness focuses on the following:

- Business Potential
- Financial Potential
- Market Potential
- Investment Potential

These four types of potential are typically what a buyer will look for at first glance before looking at your business in more detail from the inside.

Let us look at each of these four business attractiveness areas in more detail.

Business Potential

A buyer will usually look at your digital footprint. They will seek to understand what position you are aiming to occupy within your market or sector. Are your products or services clearly defined, and are they communicated in your marketing, sales strategy and brand story?

During this process, a buyer will look at your website, social media profiles, etc., and get a feel for your customer journey. This is normally the starting point for any buyer looking to acquire a business. They will want to understand your story and what value you are providing to your customers.

Another way that buyers are able to assess your business's attractiveness is to look at your online customer reviews and feedback. What is the tone of the feedback and how is any negative feedback addressed and resolved? This will say a lot about you and the strength of your brand.

In the digital age in which we live, our online presence has now become our shop window to the world, so it is important that this outward-facing part of your business is always up to date.

Financial Potential

Buyers are very often looking at several opportunities at any given time, so they will very quickly assess how well your company is doing based upon the level and quality of financial information you provide to them.

It is very rare for any small- or medium-sized business to provide anything other than the typical profit and loss and balance sheet statements. Cash flow statements and forecasts are uncommon, so if you are able to provide these, you will stand out from the crowd.

If you are able to provide a buyer with enhanced financial management reports, it will speed up their initial due diligence process and also show them that your financials are being monitored, giving any buyer a lot more confidence in your business.

The huge leap in cloud computing and digital accounting has made creating reports and monitoring business financials easier, quicker and cheaper than ever before. So, look to use all the tools available to you to create the best possible impression for a potential buyer.

Marketing Potential

Buyers will always look at sector growth to determine if your business is something in which they want to be involved. They will want to know:

- What will your sector look like in three to five years' time?
- How is your sector performing within the economy?
- Are there any barriers to entry in your sector? (The more barriers, the more attractive your business is.)
- Do you have any competitive advantages over other companies in your sector?
- Are you a forerunner or market leader in your sector?
- Do you have plans to diversify your product/service offering or penetrate new market sectors?

Having the answers to these questions and having a well-written plan will appeal to many buyers.

Investment Potential

Is your business investable?

Buyers would like to see the following:

- A steady growth in revenue, profits and cash flow
- Low staff turnover
- A genuine reason for selling
- Any strategic alignment
- An experienced management team

If your business is in a volatile sector, look to see what you could do to smooth out any peaks and troughs that may exist. This could include offering an ongoing subscription service, long-term contracts or integrating new products or services to the market.

Look to create a point of difference, something that will make you stand out from the crowd and appeal to a buyer to attract their investment.

First impressions count, and it is vital to showcase your business in the best possible light. However, this is only the beginning of the story. What is displayed on the outside must also be reflected on the inside, which is the saleability of your business.

Element 2—Business Saleability Assessment

Owning an unsaleable business is equal to owning a house with subsidence or dry rot. Most buyers will be put off; only those who are confident that they can do something with the shell of the building will even consider making an offer. At the very least, owning a business in this state will have a dramatic impact on its valuation and the price that a buyer is willing to pay, taking into consideration the amount of work and investment required to prop up the business without its current owner and produce the results that they had achieved during their time working in it. This is dependent on a buyer seeing this potential and being willing to invest their time and finances. In most cases such as this, rather than buyers seeing a 'renovation opportunity', a business remains unsaleable.

What can you do as a business owner to ensure your business is saleable and will attract the right buyers at the appropriate valuation?

In order to ascertain the saleability of your business, we need to look at the areas a buyer will assess, the findings of which will determine their valuation. These areas are:

- Customers and suppliers
- Dependency
- Exit readiness
- Financial data
- Growth potential
- Housekeeping
- Reputation
- Risk
- Shareholder alignment
- Systems and operations

Let's look at each of these business saleability areas in turn.

Customers and Suppliers

The assessment of customers and suppliers attached to a business forms part of the commercial and legal due diligence.

It looks at all the contracts and agreements in place. These agreements or contracts can be between you and your customer, your supplier or a strategic partner. Each of these documents will be assessed in terms of the risk to the company and whether there are any areas that make the business vulnerable.

To ensure a positive outcome to any such assessment, have a procedure in place for each document to be reviewed and updated on an annual basis to ensure all policies and contractual arrangements remain current and valid.

Dependency

Dependency within a business is never a good thing as it increases the risk for a potential buyer.

Internal dependency refers to the running of a business being reliant on the knowledge and skills of key staff members, including the owner. Internal dependency could leave the business vulnerable to workload or knowledge gaps, should those key personnel leave. Therefore, this part of the assessment process looks at how well the staff are looked after and what processes or procedures are in place to assist with career progression, training, knowledge transfer and employee responsibility.

To minimise internal dependency, we need to ensure that knowledge, skills and responsibilities are shared amongst staff and documented in an operations manual to be easily communicated. Another factor to consider here is employee retention. According to **www.engageemployee.com**, staff engagement in most businesses is around 45%. As employers, we need to consider not only financial remuneration, but also employee work-life balance, independence, personal growth and purpose. A programme of CPD to upskill and develop all personnel will ensure all staff are trained in the knowledge and skills essential to the business, as well as form part of your employee retention strategy.

Exit Readiness

Before selling your business, you need to have a very clear understanding of what you want from the transaction. An astute buyer will not put forward an offer. It will be up to you as the seller to tell the buyer what you want. You must be able to demonstrate and justify how that valuation was calculated and what type of deal structure you would like.

This can only be done by knowing the approximate value of your business in its current state. Calculating this well in advance will allow you to determine whether that valuation will be sufficient to meet your future financial needs, and if not, you then have time to address and rectify any gaps.

If these key areas of valuation and deal structure are not thought through before marketing your business for sale, a significant amount of time could be wasted and you may be left with a financial shortfall.

Financial Data

How accurate and current is your financial data? So many companies only ever look at their accounts at year-end or several months after their actual year-end. Outdated data means that the owner cannot make informed decisions.

Every business owner must be proactive with their financial data; however, if analysing finances is not your thing, then your accountant (or someone within your organisation) should be able to step in and provide you with monthly or quarterly management accounts, including enhanced financial reporting.

There are several key performance indicators (KPIs) that a buyer will look at, such as revenue trends, gross margins, overhead trends, average transaction value, and accounts receivables. If you as the seller are not able to provide this information, it sends a very clear message that the business may not be running as efficiently as possible.

To get the most out of your business, start asking for enhanced financial reports, get a handle on key areas within your business and ensure all your financial information is current.

Growth Potential

To enhance the value, attractiveness and saleability of your business, you need to consider all aspects of growth within it. Most people default to increasing sales, but that takes a lot of time, resources and money. There are far easier ways to grow your business before you start looking for more customers.

Look at your market to find other products or services that you could include in your offering. Consider grouping various products or services together in a bundle or offering. Carry out a gap analysis to examine what customers are buying from you and ensure they know all you have to offer. It is common for customers to only know a fraction of your offering.

Find out how you can increase the number of transactions and average transaction value. All this will go a long way towards improving your revenue and bottom line.

Assess your customer retention and service ratings to look for potential improvements. It is far easier to market to an existing customer than it is to recruit a new one.

Housekeeping

This is basic organisation, but it can be difficult to implement in practise. It is so easy for the busyness of business to take over and for the general housekeeping to be forgotten.

Housekeeping looks at all of a company's documentation. Have you got all IP, trademarks, leases, contracts, tax and VAT returns to hand, and are they up to date? All this information should be kept in a central location where it can be updated and checked on a yearly basis. What you do not want to happen is for a building lease to expire in two years' time or for your employment contracts to be out of date; scenarios such as these could be a huge risk to a buyer, and they can easily happen due to a lack of organisation.

Delegate this responsibility to someone either within the company or contracted out so that it is their duty to carry out regular checks and updates to all these documents.

Reputation

Company reputation and brand recognition is something a buyer will look at, sometimes before they even speak with a seller. Customer feedback, reviews and testimonials will go a long way towards showing a buyer that the company is well regarded and has customer loyalty.

Buyers want to know who you are and what problems you are trying to solve for your customers. Remember: Customers are only interested in how you can make their life better, safer or more efficient. What outcomes do your customers achieve by working with you? Do you know your customers' needs and are you able to satisfy them?

It is very important to increase your reputation by having several touch points with your customers throughout the year in order for you to understand their needs and for them to get to know, like and trust you.

Risk

The biggest risk facing an SME owner is owner dependency. That is why having a strong, well-motivated workforce plays a vital part in reducing the company's reliance upon its owner.

To move towards reducing a company's dependency upon its owner, manuals detailing all the systems, procedures and processes required to run the business need to be in place. As the business grows, a management team should take over the day-to-day running of the business, but the sooner the initial culture and infrastructure can be in place, the smoother the transition from owner to management team will be. To develop this culture and create a positive atmosphere within the workplace requires strong leadership, both from the owner and the subsequent management team.

Shareholder Alignment

Some businesses have multiple shareholders who own and run the business. If you are a small business, you may have formed the company many years ago with your spouse/business partner as the other shareholders. In some very unfortunate situations, there may be a divorce or separation, and in these circumstances, not having a shareholders' agreement in place can make things very difficult and costly. Whatever the make-up of your business partnership, it is always best to consider all potential scenarios in advance and put something in place to document how all parties will handle any possible future outcome.

In terms of preparing the business for sale, all major shareholders should be consulted and all agreements should be made in relation to timeframes, valuation, deal structure and type of buyer, etc.

It is worth investing in a good shareholders' agreement that will consider the various possible future scenarios. Ensure that this agreement is kept up to date with any changes as the business grows and develops.

Systems and Operations

An important part of a company's systems and operations is the marketing function, and it is crucial to keep track of which types of marketing are successful, along with their corresponding return on investment. This also includes keeping accurate databases, CRM systems, stock management and processes to follow up on quotes or tenders. All these systems and more will determine the effectiveness of the company in generating sales and retaining and acquiring customers, along with effective budgeting.

By continually focussing on your business attractiveness (what your business looks like from the outside) as well as your business saleability (what your business looks like from the inside), when the time comes to sell, this will enable a deal to progress. Once a buyer is happy with what they have seen, confident that there is potential and has weighed up the risks, they will move onto the next stage: valuation.

Element 3—Business Valuation: Transferable and Financial Valuations

Now that we've discussed the first two elements of the Value Assessment for your business (business attractiveness and business saleability) we move to the third element: business valuation. Remember: The goal of the Value Assessment is to gain Clarity on the current position of your business so that you can then determine the changes you need to make over time to get it exit ready and provide you with as many options as possible. The third element, business valuation, is integral to the exit planning process as at the end of the day, the valuation that is placed upon your business will be key to you being able to exit successfully and step into whatever it is that you have planned for your life post exit.

We briefly looked at business valuation in chapter 3, where we introduced the two elements that need to be taken into consideration when valuing an SME: transferable value and financial value. Financial value always follows transferable value, and to demonstrate this point, we looked at the four barrels:

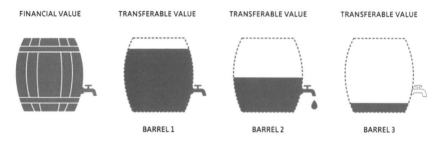

| FINANCIAL VALUE | TRANSFERABLE VALUE | TRANSFERABLE VALUE | TRANSFERABLE VALUE |

| | BARREL 1 | BARREL 2 | BARREL 3 |

Let's now look at each element in more detail:

Transferable Value

Transferable value is what a business is worth to a buyer without its previous owner. In other words, it is determined by how well the business runs without that owner. If the owner is the only person with the skills to produce the products/services or they are responsible for 90% of the company's sales, what will happen when they leave? In this section, we'll examine some key areas that buyers will assess to determine how attractive your business really is.

Transferable value should not be confused with profit either. Just because a company generates hundreds of thousands of pounds in profit each year, it does not necessarily mean it has transferable value.

Unfortunately, business owners aren't always aware that transferable value is more than a formula involving multiples of earnings or revenue, nor is it about discounted future cash flows. To really work out how much transferable value is in your business, imagine you go on holiday for three to six months and leave your laptop and mobile phone at the office. What would happen?

- How would your business perform without you?
- Would your business be able to continue with minimal disruption to its cash flow?

- Who would be responsible for running the business?
- Would the business improve?
- What weaknesses in the business would start to show?

The next step is to determine what you're spending your time doing and which tasks could be delegated. To do this, take the CEO test in chapter 4 and find out where you're spending most of your time.

Financial Value

You must find a way of cutting through the emotion and differing requirements in order to determine the value of your business based solely on facts – facts that no one can argue or dispute and that meets a buyer's three basic needs (given below). Doing this avoids emotional entanglement. Valuing a business can be complex, and there are several ways in which it can be done. In most valuation methods, there is an element of negotiation with differing views between buyer and seller, which is both the beauty and the challenge of acquisitions and negotiations.

Your business must satisfy every buyer's three basic needs:

1. The buyer must receive a return on their investment.
2. The buyer must be able to replicate or improve the results of the current owner.
3. The business must be able to pay off its debts.

Would your business allow a buyer to do this?

If it would, then you are well on your way to having a saleable business.

If it would not, then you need to take a step back, reassess and recognise that you need to make changes now to ensure that those basic buyer needs can be met. By ensuring your business meets the three basic needs of a buyer, you'll naturally increase not only the value of your business, but also its saleability. In addition, should the worst case happen where you have to sell quickly, you'll be much better placed to appeal to as many buyers as possible and ready for a swift sales process.

At the very minimum, your business needs to generate sufficient cash flow, which ideally should be as close to your net profit figure as possible, to provide a buyer with a return on any money they invest in the business as well as service any debt required to purchase or run the business. This could be in the form of asset finance, debt finance, deferred payments, etc. If your business is unable to do that, then it is very possible that your business valuation is too high, based upon the cash flow generated by the business.

So how do we go about valuing a business?

Financial Valuation Methods

The seven methods I tend to use are:

- Balance sheet valuation
- Discounted cash flow (DCF)
- Multiple of EBITDA
- Multiple of recurring revenue
- Return on investment
- Cash payback
- Cash flow valuation

In order to achieve a balanced valuation of any business, I always use, and would encourage you to use, at least three valuation methods. This creates a balanced view, providing a valuation range and a valuation weighting, giving you a good all-round picture of the business.

The three I use most often are:

- Multiple of EBITDA or multiple of recurring revenue (whichever is more applicable)
- Return on investment
- Cash flow valuation

Why not balance sheet valuation? The value of the balance sheet has little bearing on most SMEs, unless the owner wants to liquidate the business or there are some high-ticket items involved, such as property, plant or machinery. For most SMEs, there won't be much in the way of tangible assets such as these.

Why not discounted cash flow (DFC)? DFC is typically used in much larger corporations because with larger businesses, the future is more predictable when compared to a general SME. However, this method could be used if the SME has a few long-term contracts or has a subscription-based model.

Before further discussing my three preferred methods – multiples of EBITDA or multiple of earnings, return on investment and cash flow valuation – let me warn you that in any deal, there will probably be an element of disagreement where the seller fixes on the highest valuation number and the buyer fixes on the lowest valuation. However, focusing solely on the numbers and removing any emotional attachment to the business should make negotiations easier.

Each buyer will view what your business will be worth to them based upon their own situation and their personal requirements. As a seller, you will have little control over which buyer will consider your business or how they will value it. This is all very subjective and could result in you being offered more for your business than you were expecting, but equally, you could be offered less.

My aim here is to give you, the seller, some control over this process; for you to determine the value of your business so that buyers cannot argue against it or disagree with you about it. One of the keys to valuing a business is being able to show a buyer how you got to your valuation and being able to clearly justify why you are valuing your business at that amount. All too often, sellers tell me how much they want for their business but are unable to demonstrate how they have calculated their valuation, which tends to lead to the deal collapsing.

NOTE: This is why it is so important that the Value Assessment looks not only at your business plan but also your personal and financial plans (which we will address in chapters 7 and 8). It is only through combining these three plans – by knowing exactly where you are and what and where your target destination is – that you will be able to know what your business needs to be worth in order to achieve your goals and, more importantly, when those goals have been achieved. Through the Value Assessment, you will know exactly the amount you need to sell the business for and can confidently show any buyer how that valuation was calculated.

The first step to a financial valuation is to understand the profitability of your business. In some industries, revenue is used to value a business; for others, net profit is used, but the proof of any business is whether it can make money – in other words, can it generate positive cash flow?

Multiple of EBITDA or Multiple of Recurring Revenue

Depending on the sector in which the business operates, the multiples based on an EBITDA or recurring revenue can vary significantly.

To give you an example:

Multiple of EBITDA			Multiple of Recurring Revenue		
EBITDA:		£100,000	Recurring Revenue:		£400,000
Agreed Multiple of:	x	3.5	Agreed Multiple of:	x	1.1
Business Valuation:		**£350,000**	**Business Valuation:**		**£440,000**

NOTE: Even if you are using a multiple of recurring revenues to calculate the business valuation, it will still be very dependent on how profitable the business is. Remember the three needs of every buyer: the return on investment, the ability to replicate the owners results and the ability to service any debt. If this business with a valuation of £440,000 is only producing £20,000 in net profit, then that valuation will not make financial sense and is far too high, unless of course there are extenuating circumstances at play, such as intellectual property, trademarks, products, or services that will be valuable to a buyer and can command such a valuation.

Return on Investment

This method is based upon the annual return a prospective buyer would look to generate from the investment. This will differ between buyers, but the typical ROI will be between 25% and 35%.

To give you an example:

EBITDA:	£100,000
Assume ROI of:	35%
Business Valuation:	**£285,714**

Cash Flow Valuation

The method that I am going to share with you now calculates the value of your business based solely on its performance, which as the seller, you control. It works in a similar way to how a bank would assess your ability to pay back a loan or a mortgage. This method acts as a sanity check to ensure the valuation placed on the business is realistic and should appeal to the widest possible audience of buyers.

This method is called the cash flow valuation method. The reason it is called the 'cash flow' valuation method is because it uses the cash flow generated by the business to calculate its value. The primary reason for acquisitions is to purchase the cash flow generated by a business, which, in theory, should be as close to the net profit figure as possible, providing the business has a handle on the six keys that control cash flow: debtor days, creditor days, stock days, expenses, cost of goods sold (COGS) and sales. You can read more about gaining control of these six keys of cash flow in my book, The Cash Flow Code. I have also created an online tool called the Cash Flow Simulator, which can be used to calculate and assess your cash flow and measure how changes to the six keys will impact future cash flow. For free access to this tool, please visit **www.thesmarterexit.com**.

The cash flow valuation method is a valuation method that I have developed and, as such, is not freely available through any other source. If you would like to value your business based upon the cash flow that it generates, please contact me at **hello@businessbydesign.co.uk** and I will be pleased to work with you.

When using this valuation method, you will be asked to input four numbers:

1. The company's EBITDA, or you can use net profit if you do not have the EBITDA to hand.

2. Any tangible assets the business may have, i.e., vehicles, plant, machinery, anything a buyer could use to obtain asset finance on.

3. If there is any debt in the business, it will need to be included here.

4. Then you need to enter an amount, or the market rate, that would represent how much it would cost to replace you (the owner) with a manager and/or employee(s) to carry out all the work you do within the business.

Regarding the fourth input, this could be a rather complex question in itself which requires further clarification. If you have no involvement in the business at all, then this amount will be zero. This zero amount may apply to you, but it will not apply for the vast majority of owners. Let me explain why.

As the owner of your business, I suspect you wear a number of different hats and probably do the work of at least two or three people. Take a sober look at everything you do within your business and determine how many people you would realistically need to hire to replace yourself in the business. For example: you may need to hire a branch manager and the going salary for that position could be around £40,000 per annum (pa). You may need to also hire an administrator at a salary of around £15,000 pa. It could be an engineer, an operational manager or any person or people that would be needed to carry out all the work you currently do within your business. Add up all these salaries and the total figure will be what is placed in the last box of the cash flow valuation.

The advantage of using the cash flow valuation method is that it is objective; it removes any emotions and opinions from the valuation and looks at the harsh reality of how the business is performing. Although this way of calculating the value of your business may seem inaccurate or unfair, it does take into account the worst-case scenario: if you had to sell the business quickly. However, this method does leave you as the business owner in complete control because you, and only you, are responsible for your company's results. If the value of the business is not where you need it to be, you can examine your business to identify how you can reduce the company's debt, how you could increase its profits, and how you can work towards removing yourself from the day-to-day operation of the business. As we looked at in part one of this book, this will be the shift from your business being owner centric to being value centric.

The good news is that you are in control. Improving your cash flow and/or the net profit your business generates will improve your business's financial valuation, as well as your ability to sell it. By changing your results, you change the saleability of your business, not only giving you the most options available for your future, but also the best returns on your investment in the present time up to your future exit.

Tip: Reported Net Profit vs True Net Profit

Warning: *You must remove yourself from the day-to-day running of your business before you sell or else it will affect your ability to sell or achieve the valuation you want. Buyers aren't looking for jobs, meaning they aren't looking to become the head worker of your business. They want managers already in place – managers with a proven track record to run the business.*

The difference between reported net profit and true net profit is what catches a lot of business owners out. They tend to be owners who are heavily involved in the business. It is one of the major reasons why initial valuations are reduced by tens of thousands – because reported net profit is not the same as true net profit.

Reported net profit is the figure that you see at the bottom of your profit and loss statement (income statement). It is the figure that shows whether your business has made a profit or a loss.

For you to gain an understanding of true net profit, let me use an example to explain. Let's assume you have a business producing £100k net profit. As the owner, you work five days a week in the business and are crucial to the success and day-to-day running of the company. You may assume that, if you were to sell your business today, you could expect a multiple of 3 x profit. Using our simplified example, this would give you a valuation of £300k.

Along comes a buyer who asks you some key questions about your business, starting with this one: What is your involvement in the day-to-day running of the business?

It is best to be honest here as the truth will come out anyway during the due diligence phase. You tell the buyer that you work five days a week and are fairly involved in the running of the business.

This then leads to series of other questions:

- What roles do you perform?
- How many members of staff do you think you would need to replace the work you do?
- What do you think would be a reasonable salary to offer these members of staff?

Now, as the owner, you will do a lot more work than the average employee, so you reckon that the buyer would probably need a manager at a salary of £40k and an administrator at £20k to take care of all the organisational tasks you have inherited over time.

Assuming we use a multiple of 3 x profit, you have just wiped £180k from the initial valuation.

How did that happen?

You see, your reported net profit of £100k was not the true net profit. Because you are intrinsically involved in the business, the buyer would either need to assume the role of manager or employ a manager at £40k, as well as an administrator at £20k, which in total would reduce the net profit by £60k, resulting in a true net profit figure of £40k. If you were to then use the multiple of 3x profit, this will give your business a valuation of £120k.

However, if we use the same scenario with the reported net profit of £100k but this time with a manager and administrator already in place, the reported net profit and true net profit would be the same number, resulting in the valuation of £300k being correct.

Therefore, it is absolutely imperative to remove yourself from the day-to-day running of your business and to build a team around you. Surrounding yourself with key people won't only add value to your business, but will also reduce your workload, increase your work-life balance and give you peace of mind that your business can run without you should you need to take time off, thus making your life a whole lot easier and enjoyable during the years leading up to your eventual exit.

In the end, an SME is worth:

- What owners are willing to sell for
- What buyers are willing to pay

The key here is to know exactly what you are willing to sell your business for. You can only know this by having a financial plan and knowing 'Your Number', which is the amount of money you will need in order to retire and live the lifestyle you want without the fear of ever running out of money (we cover this in detail later in the book).

To understand what buyers are willing to pay, you can use valuation methods such as those discussed earlier. They can act as a reference point to give you an idea of the value of your business, which can then be used as a potential starting point for negotiations.

For many small-business owners, this valuation is the result of years of the hard work and sacrifice it took to create a successful venture, so it makes sense to get the best possible return for everything you have invested.

Element 4—Financial Due Diligence and Benchmarking

To help you gain Clarity of your business, after the first three elements of the Value Assessment – business attractiveness, business saleability and valuation – comes the fourth element: financial due diligence and benchmarking. In addition to determining the value of your business using at least three evaluation methods, including the cash flow valuation method, you should carry out a financial due diligence of your business's performance over the last three years. This will provide a full 360-degree view and show you what is really happening within your business from a financial perspective. It will give you the opportunity to view your business through the eyes of a buyer. A buyer will typically look at and undertake the following analyses.

- Revenue analysis
- Customer analysis
- Margin analysis
- Overhead analysis
- Net profit analysis
- Fixed asset analysis
- Net current asset analysis
- Cash and stock analysis
- Detailed balance sheet analysis
- Supplier analysis
- Sales channel analysis

During these analyses, a buyer will focus on the trends in your business from the last three years and project these forward to determine what your business will look like in one-, two-, or three-years' time. Doing this will highlight any potential risks or dependencies within the business that could render it vulnerable. A buyer will examine cycles to determine, for example, if there may be any cash or revenue gaps during a financial year. All these elements will start to create a picture for a buyer, allowing them to weigh up whether or not the acquisition of your business is worth pursuing.

On the other hand, if you as the seller are able to compile this document of analyses long before you need or want to exit, it will give you a very good handle on how your business appears to the outside world and enable you to address any areas of vulnerability before they are identified by a potential buyer.

Benchmarking

It is also incredibly helpful to compare your results (for the metrics given below) to that of the industry or sector averages, which is called 'benchmarking'. This allows you to determine how well your business is performing among other companies in your sector. If your business is underperforming, you'll know where to improve, as well as what potential increase in your business financial valuation can be achieved, should certain areas within your business be addressed or improved.

The typical averages used for benchmarking are:
- Gross profit margin (%)
- Operating profit margin (%)
- Profit before interest and tax margin (%)
- Pre-tax profit margin (%)
- Return on total assets (%)
- Return on capital employed (%)
- Return on equity (%)
- Current ratio
- Quick ratio
- Debt ratio
- Credit given (days)
- Credit taken (days)
- Times interest earned

- Fixed asset turnover
- Stock turnover
- Debtor turnover
- Turnover per employee (£)
- Average wage (£)
- Turnover growth (%)
- Operating profit growth (%)

With these metrics, you'll be able to compare your company's performance to that of others in your sector and evaluate whether your business is performing above, at or below the industry averages. This will determine if there is room for improvement and if so, where that improvement needs to happen.

The aim here is for you to gain a greater understanding of how your business is currently performing, what your business is worth from a financial point of view and how to make your business more saleable to a buyer. During the interim, you'll most likely be also improving the profitability of your business.

> **NOTE:** Benchmarking is not an exact science. The information gathered by data agencies are not always accurate, especially when it comes to SMEs. However, it does serve as a useful guide and gives you some indication of how your business is performing.

Element 5—Exit and Buyer Analysis

Here we arrive at the fifth and final element for the Value Assessment of your business: the exit and buyer analysis. As part of creating an exit strategy, we need to assess the type of exit you are looking to achieve, which is the exit analysis. Also, if in your exit analysis you determine that you'll be selling in the future, you'll need to do a buyer analysis to determine who your target buyer is likely to be.

As for an exit analysis, there are potentially three types of exits from which you can choose:

- Sell
- Liquidation
- Close down

Let's look at each of these three types in turn.

Sell

If you are wanting to sell, you then need to undertake a buyer analysis, which we will discuss later in this chapter.

Liquidation

I know for a lot of people the word 'liquidation' conjures up a lot of negative connotations and is very often seen as a sign of failure. However, please note that there are two types of liquidation:

- Unplanned liquidation
- Planned liquidation

Unplanned liquidation is bad and is often seen as a sign of failure. It typically occurs when the owner suddenly becomes ill, disabled or dies and there is no effective succession plan in place. Unplanned liquidation can also occur when the business becomes insolvent and unable to pay its debts. Generally, unplanned liquidation is a worst-case scenario, affecting not only the owner, but their family, employees and creditors.

Planned or voluntary liquidation, if done in the right way, is a very reasonable way to exit a business for certain sectors, and it is not a sign of failure. This method is used if a company is looking to cease trading. For shareholders, this may be an appropriate exit strategy since there may be some tax-efficiencies, if applicable. This method is also applicable if there is no option of selling the business due to the risk levels for a buyer, making it an unviable sale. In this scenario, liquidating the assets is often the best or perhaps the only feasible method of exiting the business.

The process of liquidating a business is the conversion of assets into cash by selling them to a user or consumer. There are generally three categories of business that will liquidate assets:

- *Assets indirectly used for creating an income:* This includes the furniture, fixtures and equipment (FFE) for typical service based businesses.
- *Assets used as tools in the direct creation of income:* These assets would be sold to similar types of businesses, typically in the manufacturing and construction sectors.

- *Assets that directly create an income:* These are typically the stock from retail businesses such as Blockbuster, Toys "R" Us and Debenhams, for example.

To achieve the best results, liquidation must be done in the right way and there are firms available to assist with this. It is also important, and morally right, to note that with planned liquidation, all debts should be settled and all employees looked after. It would also be advisable to seek professional help to ensure that everything is done correctly.

Close Down

After selling and liquidation, the third type of exit is for a business to simply close down. This only becomes an option if the business cannot be sold due to the level of risk a buyer would have to take on or if the business cannot be liquidated due to the lack of assets. If an owner knows early on that closure is a potential exit route, it will allow them to use their business in such a way so as to fund their personal and financial plans in the most tax-efficient way during the life of the business. This will be a long-term plan to strategically grow and develop the business in order for it to generate healthy profits, which are then taken out of the business to be used in other investment vehicles. These investments are then used to help bridge any wealth gaps the owner may have at exit.

Buyer Analysis

In order to be as prepared as possible for your exit and to know what you are working towards, you need to understand what your preferred type of exit will be, and if that preferred exit method is to sell, it is beneficial to then understand which type of buyer you would be looking to sell to. Understanding this will help you to prepare your business in the best way for that buyer type so that when the time comes to market, you will be ready to attract the type of buyer that you are looking for. You can ascertain which type of buyer would be best suited to your business and your future plans by carrying out a buyer analysis.

When it comes to selling, there are two broad options available to you as a business owner: you could look for a buyer outside of your business or you could look internally. Within these two broad options, each buyer type will have their own unique set of advantages and disadvantages. Knowing what these are will allow you to make informed choices and put the necessary plans into place.

The options for an external buyer or exit are:
• IPO (Initial Public Offering)
• PEG (Private Equity Groups)
• Strategic or Trade Buyers
• Financial or Private Investors

The options for an internal buyer or exit are:
• Family
• Business Partner or Shareholder
• Management Buyout
• Employee Ownership

The option you choose will depend on what is important to you. There is no right or wrong option here; it purely comes down to what you want out of the exit, the type of legacy you wish to leave behind and the tax benefits available to you.

Externally

First, let us look at the types of external buyers. Each buyer type will view your business differently and certain aspects will be more pertinent to them than others.

There are generally four types of external buyers, each with their own individual set of risks, goals and financial means:
• Initial Public Offering (IPO)
• Private Equity Groups (PEGs)
• Strategic or Trade Buyers
• Private Investors

For the rest of this section, we'll look at these four types of buyers in turn and their sets of risks, goals and financial means so that you can gain an overall understanding of the buyer types and start to consider which would be best suited to your business and future plans.

External Buyer Type 1: Initial Public Offering

An Initial Public Offering will only apply to a very small number of SMEs who go on to reach unicorn status, where their value is greater than £500m. As this type of exit is outside the remit of this book, we will not go into too much detail, but I wanted to include it as it is a method of exiting a business. According to IG.com, the IPO process starts when a company decides that it wants to sell its shares to the public via a stock exchange. First, an audit must be conducted, which considers all aspects of a company's financials. If everything is in order, the business then has to prepare a registration statement to file with the appropriate exchange commission, like the Securities and Exchange Commission (SEC) in the US or the Financial Conduct Authority (FCA) in the UK.

Next, the stock exchange on which the company wants to list will review the application, after which it is either accepted – sometimes subject to certain amendments – or rejected. If it is approved, the company will enlist the help of an underwriter to help it decide how many shares to issue and at what price. The underwriter is usually a bank, and it is their job to start a book-building process, looking for investors to subscribe to (register their interest in) the IPO. Any interested parties will receive a prospectus of information detailing the shares where they will be listed along with the potential opening price.

The IPO will be the first chance for non-private investors to buy the company's shares in what is known as the primary market – a transaction between the original holder (the company) and an investor.

Previously, there have been restrictions on IPOs that meant that only institutional investors could participate fully in this primary market, while retail investors could only participate in the secondary market (when shares are exchanged between investors). However, there is now a mechanism where retail investors can invest at the same time and price as institutional investors.

As previously stated, this exit method will only apply to a select few.

External Buyer Type 2: Private Equity Groups

Private equity groups (PEGs) are typically investment management companies that provide financial backing and make investments in the private equity of start-up or operating companies. They want to realise a return on their investment within five to seven years through a sale or initial public offering (IPO). PEGs usually split their acquisitions into two groups:

- Platforms
- Add-ons

Platforms are acquisitions into sectors where PEGs do not already operate. These are stand-alone transactions with no synergies, and the aim is to grow the acquired business for a return. They create value through operating partnerships, capital infusions and possibly add-ons to explore avenues for growth to increase the chance of a successful investment.

Some key buyer questions for platform acquisitions include the following:

- How attractive is this industry?
- Does the business have multiple avenues of growth?
- How can value be added?
- What is an acceptable risk-adjusted return?

Companies that are acquired typically have sales of £10m or more.

Add-ons are acquisitions into sectors where PEGs already operate. The PEG's focus is more on the strategic and financial benefits of adding to their existing portfolio of companies. The acquisition serves a specific purpose in either geography, new products, complementary customer base, economies of scale, etc.

Some key buyer questions for add-on acquisitions are:

- How does this acquisition support the platform company?
- What are the synergies, and will it make the overall offering more valuable?
- What is an acceptable return on capital?

Companies that are acquired typically, but not always, have sales of £5m or more.

As the owner, you will need to be aware of these differences in perspective because they have a significant impact on how PEGs will view your business and what they are willing to pay. If it is an add-on investment, there will need to be some synergies. If it is a platform investment, there needs to be evidence of growth, as well as a growth plan for the future.

Advantages of a PEG Buyer:

- They have significant financial backing.
- They may contract you into the business for a period after the acquisition – an advantage if you would still like to be part of the business.
- They have the resources to grow the business.

Disadvantages of a PEG Buyer:

- They may contract you into the business for a period after the acquisition – a disadvantage if you want to walk away straight after the handover period.
- They tend to take a long time to complete an acquisition.
- There is a higher risk of staff, customers or suppliers hearing about the sale too early in the process.
- It can get extremely expensive in terms of legal and personal time.
- Staff could lose their jobs.

If you as the owner are staying with the business after selling, you need to understand what the new organisational structure will be like and how much scrutiny to expect from the PEG. Platform investments will likely get more attention, whereas add-on investments might see more oversight from the parent company rather than the PEG itself. If you are keeping an equity stake, it is important to understand what a PEG plans to do with the business because, in this scenario, they are more of a partner than an investor.

External Buyer Type 3—Strategic or Trade Buyers

Strategic or trade buyers tend to place more emphasis on non-financial assets. They identify companies whose products or services can synergistically integrate with their existing offering, such as new technology, new products, production methods, etc. These buyers can also be unrelated to your company but are looking to grow within your market in order to diversify their revenue sources.

Strategic or trade buyers primarily differ in four ways when compared to PEGs in terms of:

1) valuation
2) return on investment
3) industry
4) infrastructure.

Let's briefly look at these four differences.

1) Valuation: Strategic or trade buyers focus heavily on synergies and integration capabilities while PEGs look at cash-generating capability and growth potential.

Some key questions strategic or trade buyers typically ask include the following:

- Do your products or services complement what they offer?
- Does your company serve a new/different customer segment?
- Are there manufacturing economies of scale they can realise?
- Are there intellectual property or trade secrets that you have developed that they want to own or prevent a competitor from owning?

2) Return on Investment: Strategic or trade buyers plan to keep newly acquired businesses for the foreseeable future. PEGs typically have an investment time horizon of only five to seven years. This will impact how much each is willing to pay for your business. PEGs are a lot more sensitive to economic cycles and will often take this into account in their valuation of a business.

3) Industry: Strategic or trade buyers know the industry and, thus, focus more of their time in determining how your business can integrate with their overall strategy. Conversely, PEGs focus on both your business and the industry in which they operate. For industries that are highly regulated or unpredictable, finding a strategic or trade buyer can help to reduce those associated risks as they are already aware of these regulations and tend to be easier to deal with.

4) *Infrastructure*: Strategic or trade buyers tend to focus less on how well developed the target company's operational infrastructure is, i.e., IT, HR, legal, etc. as they will already have these functions within their own operation. PEGs generally do not have these functions in place. As a result, they will scrutinise operational infrastructure during the due diligence process and often seek to bolster this post acquisition.

Advantages of Strategic or Trade Buyers:
- They know the industry.
- They can leverage their own company to finance the acquisition.
- They may contract you into the business for a period after the acquisition – an advantage if you would still like to be part of the business.
- They have the resources to grow the business.
- The acquisitions tend to be a little quicker when compared to PEGs.

Disadvantages of Strategic or Trade Buyers:
- They are not after your business itself but only what the business can provide.
- There is a greater chance of staff job losses.
- They may contract you into the business for a period after the acquisition – a disadvantage if you simply want to walk away after the handover period.

External Buyer Type 4: Private Investors

A private investor could be a company or an individual who invests in businesses that have typically been operating for five years or more. This period can be less than five years, but the lack of trading history may make the acquisition a little riskier and therefore drive down the valuation.

The general target acquisition profile is a company with profits of between £50k to £750k, bearing in mind that the amount of work and costs to acquire a company with profits of £100k is not significantly different to a company with profits of £1m.

A private investor would be looking for a management team to be in place with a proven history of sales and profit growth. Their general remit is one of letting the management team run the business while they will look for opportunities to improve efficiencies, economies of scale and growth. As in my own case, as this is the type of business buyer I am, the aim for a private investor may be to acquire a number of companies in the same sector in order to create a group. These investors are not interested in the day-to-day running of the business but more in running and leading the group.

This type of investor tends to make up the largest part of the four investor groups. If your aim is to make your business attractive to as many people as possible, this is the group to aim for. Should you target this group of investors, this will inevitably make your business attractive to the other three investor groups as well.

Private investors will base their valuation on a business's historic performance and the amount of EBITDA. Future potential of the business plays almost no role in the valuation as this potential will need to be realised by the investor themselves, although some future potential will make the business more saleable.

Private investors may know nothing about your industry. This may cause some business owners to write these investors off and be reluctant to sell to them, but I urge you not to be too hasty. As I can personally attest is true for me as a private investor, these investors tend to surround themselves with a team of experts or are able to call upon people who do know the industry. I have personally bought a number of companies knowing nothing about their industry sector but have had people around me whom I could draft in, should the need arise. This ought to be viewed as a positive because they will approach everything with a fresh pair of eyes, often finding innovative ways of working that may not occur to someone who has been in the industry for several years.

Deal structure will play a large part in the private investor's strategy as this will make the acquisition possible. Most business owners have only one type of deal structure in mind, whereas a private investor may have many. Therefore, you will need to ensure you are aware of the scope of potential deal structures in readiness for being open to an offer.

Advantages of a Private Investor Buyer:
- They can move very quickly.
- They will ensure the process remains confidential.
- They intend to keep as many staff as possible.
- They will look to grow the business and keep your legacy.
- They are the largest of the four groups of investors.

Disadvantages of a Private Investor Buyer:
- They will not write a cheque for the full valuation of the business on completion.
- They will require finance, be it using personal, asset, debt or vendor finance.
- There may be a six- to 12-month handover period.

Internally

An internal transfer of ownership is usually preferred by some owners as a more popular option. This is usually driven by the type of legacy they wish to leave, tax implications and how quickly they need to exit.

Also, an internal transfer is normally more confidential and requires additional pre-planning as there will be certain elements that would need to be in place, so it will give the owner more options for whatever the future brings.

There are generally four types of internal transfers that can take place:

- Sell to a family member(s)
- Sell to a business partner or shareholder
- Sell to management
- Sell to employees

Sell to a Family Member(s)

Working with family is tricky; I have first-hand experience of this. There are so many dynamics at play, so many moving parts, so many pitfalls.

The first part, as with any exit strategy, is for the exiting family member(s) to know exactly what *Their Number* is. **Their Number** is the amount of money needed at retirement to live the lifestyle they want – most of the time this number is not known, and without first having this knowledge, business owners are simply walking blind.

From my experience in consulting with family-run businesses, there are generally two major issues that need to be addressed:

• Communication
• Ability & Motivation

Communication:

The first problem area I often notice is a lack of communication – between parents and children, between siblings, between the family and their employees.

I tend to see a lot of assumptions being made, sometimes through sheer miscommunication or the fear of facing reality or the 'elephant in the room'. Part of the reason for these assumptions and fear is that the owners – normally the parents – assume that their child or children will take over the running of the business, but they have never actually discussed it, or at least have not discussed it in any depth. This may be through ignorance, but sometimes it is through fear of not wanting to hear that their child or children do not want to take over the business they have worked so hard to build over many years.

Ability & Motivation

The next big question is to look at whether the younger generation have the ability and motivation to actually run the business. There are occasions where the child/children are really good at what they do within the business, but they do not possess the ability and acumen to run the business itself.

I know of an owner, John, who was planning to exit his business within the next five to seven years. He had built and grown the business over several decades and was relatively successful. However, he made the cardinal sin of building a business in such a way that it was dependent upon him, and this made the business unsaleable. Coming to that realisation, he opted for what he believed to be the best course of action, which was to give the business to his daughter, Sarah, to run. As she already worked in the business, all John had to do was to train Sarah to run the business and, over the course of the five-to-seven-year period, he would slowly step away, handing the reigns over to Sarah. He would remain a shareholder and director and take an annual dividend or salary of around £35,000 to fund his retirement.

Sounds like a feasible plan...

The problem was that Sarah did not know anything about this, and although she was working in the business and enjoyed working with her dad, she did not view it as a permanent career for herself. However, after some lengthy private discussions between John and Sarah, she understood the opportunity and was happy to make a go of the business.

I was informed of their decision, and I raised a few more concerns in the form of realistic scenarios that could play out which, if the business was unprepared for these potential events, would leave John in a very unfortunate predicament.

The first area that needed to be addressed was the other members of staff. Sarah is a highly intelligent person and a good leader, so it was well within her ability to learn to run the business. What they also needed to factor in was to bring the two senior members of staff into the discussion and involve them in the process. This would give Sarah the backing and support needed and bring a further depth of experience and wisdom to the team. There was also a discussion between John and Sarah as to whether there was any merit in including these two senior staff members, along with Sarah, as owners and shareholders of the business, as this would certainly take the pressure off Sarah as well as incentivise the two employees.

The other area of concern was John's personal financials. Understanding that there was little saleable value within his business was a step in the right direction and his idea of simply taking £35,000 per year from the business seemed reasonable. However, it was severely floored for a number of reasons.

Let us look at a few 'What If' scenarios:

- What if in 10 years' time Sarah becomes seriously ill or injured and can no longer work?

- What if Sarah dies before John?
- What if Sarah wants to have children and be a stay-at-home parent for a while?
- What if Sarah decides the business is not for her and packs it in or sells it for a nominal amount?
- What if Sarah starts to resent paying John the £35,000 per year when he is no longer working in the business?

These scenarios would either force John back into working in the business or leave him without the £35,000 per year. What would that look like and where would that leave him?

So, although his succession plan seemed feasible on paper, when broken down, it could potentially put both of them in a difficult position, should their lives take a turn from the way they had planned.

The option for John at this point is to create a personal financial strategy which will provide the £35,000 per year without the need to rely on the business. The next step is to create transferable value within the company as quickly as possible and, given the five-to-seven-year timeframe, this is certainly achievable. As this progresses, and if John still wants Sarah to take over the business, then he should treat Sarah as an external buyer rather than as his daughter, keeping the business and their family as separate as possible.

Sell to Business Partners/Shareholders

This is probably the easiest option because all the partners or shareholders already know and understand the business. The key to successfully exiting the business using this option is to ensure there are clear lines of communication between all parties. Ideally, these scenarios would have already been discussed and played out many years before and a framework written down in the shareholders' agreement, covering all the various scenarios that could happen and what the appropriate action will be to remedy that situation.

Having a comprehensive and up-to-date shareholders' agreement, including an arbitration clause, is imperative and I would strongly urge every business with more than one owner or shareholder to have this in place.

Sell to Management

When it comes to management ownership, there are many flavours to choose from. The flavour that will best suit you will depend on the time you have left before wanting to exit the business, the amount of control you want, the speed of acquisition, the type of deal structure best suited for you and your business and what tax implications you will have once the transaction is completed.

These options are subject to change, and when the 'powers that be' make those changes, it is always sensible to seek the advice of experts in these fields to fully understand which option will be best and most tax efficient for you at the time of wanting to sell.

I will explain just four types of management ownership options to give you an understanding of what is possible and to help you to consider which will work for you and your business.

The four types of management ownership options are:
- MBO (Management Buyout)
- MBI (Management Buy-In)
- VIMBO (Vendor Initiated Management Buyout)
- BIMBO (Buy-In Management Buyout)

MBO (Management Buyout)

Management buyouts (MBOs) are becoming an increasingly popular form of exit for both owner-managed businesses and large corporates. MBO is the purchase of a company by members of its management team. This usually happens when an owner wishes to exit the business or, in some cases, a parent company wishes to sell a part of their business.

The key benefits for owners are that they control the process, the sale is kept confidential, it is low risk and the future of the business is secured.

The key benefits for the management team are that they already understand the business and, as such, know it is a good investment and there is limited risk but there are also high returns to be had.

Key Elements:
- The company must have a track record of profitability.
- There should be a strong management team in place to ensure success.
- The owner must have a realistic expectation of the price and deal structure.
- The management team must be able to fund the initial consideration.

MBI (Management Buy-In)

The difference between management buy*out* and management buy-*in* is the position of the buyer. In the case of a management buy*out*, the buyers are already working for the target company. However, a management buy-*in* involves a purchase from outside the company; therefore, it will be a completely new team taking on the ownership and management of the business.

The target company is acquired by outside investors with a view to increase the company's performance with a new strategy and/or management team.

An MBI is seen as a riskier proposition by funders than an MBO as there may be a learning curve for the incoming management team to negotiate when they take control of the business. This perceived risk could affect their ability to secure the funding needed to facilitate such a purchase.

Key Elements:
- The target company may be undervalued.
- This would be a good option if the current owner is struggling to manage the company.
- A new management team may be able to grow the company and maximise shareholder value.
- Existing employees may be negatively impacted by this change in management.

VIMBO (Vendor Initiated Management Buyout)

A vendor-initiated management buyout (VIMBO) is a virtually identical process to a management buyout (MBO) but with one key difference: the vendor puts together a clear and organised deal before approaching the team. In other words, the vendor takes control of the process.

A finance package is typically proposed by the seller to allow the transaction to complete. This often involves using some of the company's cash resources as an immediate lump sum before using its future profits to fund the purchase on deferred terms.

The Process:
- Form a new company with employees as shareholders with agreed percentages.
- Obtain HMRC clearance to allow the continuation of the company.
- The new company buys the shares for cash and loan notes.
- The vendor remains in control until it is all paid and if the management team is not successful in running the business, the vendor has a lien on the shares to get them all back.

Key Elements:
- The company owner initiates the deal on their terms.
- Financial risk in the business is minimised.
- The business value is paid using cash or loan notes payable to the owner over several years.
- The vendor can share in any future profits and oversee the succession of the business to the management team.
- This is a good option to pass the company down to the next generation.
- A VIMBO may be a tax-efficient way of exiting a business.

BIMBO (Buy-In Management Buyout)

A BIMBO is a form of a Leveraged Buyout (LBO) that incorporates characteristics of both a Management Buyout (MBO) along with a Management Buy-In (MBI).

A BIMBO occurs when the existing management team, along with an outside management team, decide to buy out a company. The existing management represents the buyout portion while the outside managers represent the buy-in portion.

This option provides the advantages of both buy-in and buyout. Because the existing members of management are already familiar with the business, the transfer will be made more efficiently and without disruption. This management buyout is complemented with management buy-in, which results in the influx of new leaders with expertise to fill areas of need in the business: a new product or service under development, marketing, operations management or finance.

Key Elements:
*   New and existing managers must get along for the BIMBO to work.
*   Employees may take sides and conflicts may occur, as they do with any change within an organization.
*   Increase of debt on the balance sheet that must be managed responsibly by the management team.

Now that we have explored how the owner of a business can exit using its management team, in the next section, we will look at how an owner can exit a business using their employees.

Sell to Employees

In much the same way as with a Management Buyout, there are many flavours from which to choose. The benefits may change over time and certain flavours will be added, changed or removed. I would therefore encourage you to familiarise yourself with the types of options available to you and seek the advice of a specialist solicitor or tax planner to establish which option will be best suited to your situation at the time you wish to exit.

Below is a list of the most common types of options currently available. I have purposefully not gone into too much detail as they tend to change over time, but I have given enough information to give you an indication of the benefits of each.

EOT (Employee Ownership Trust)

An EOT is a form of employee benefit trust introduced by the Government in September 2014 to encourage more shareholders to set up a corporate structure, similar to the John Lewis and Partners model.

An EOT is intended to create a stable, long-term sustainability with an engaged and committed workforce.

Shareholders who sell more than 50% of the ordinary share capital in their company to an EOT can now benefit from a complete exemption from capital gains tax (CGT) in the tax year in which the EOT first acquires a majority shareholding. The aim is to facilitate wider employee-ownership via an indirect holding.

Although the tax breaks are aimed at companies, there is no reason why those businesses that are held by a partnership could not be incorporated so that, when the time comes for exit, the shareholders (former partners) can sell their shares to an EOT.

This is currently the most generous form of CGT relief for business owners, more favourable than Business Asset Disposal Relief (formerly Entrepreneurs Relief), and without the £10m lifetime cap.

Key Elements:
- Sellers can exit their business at their own pace.
- It is currently the most tax-efficient route to exit a business.
- The trust holds the shares on behalf of all employees.
- There is an annual income tax free bonus for employees.

EMI (Enterprise Management Incentive)

An EMI is a tax-advantaged share option scheme designed for smaller companies. The EMI is a share option scheme that enables companies to attract and retain key staff by rewarding them with equity participation in the business. The scheme is ideal for smaller, entrepreneurial companies that might not be able to match the salaries paid elsewhere.

The plan is extremely flexible, and options may be granted over any class of shares, with any exercise price and any performance conditions. To maximise the tax breaks, shares should not be sold for at least two years after the date the option was granted and with the price set at market value. The value of shares in a private company can be agreed upon with HMRC in advance.

Key Elements:
- It is extremely flexible.
- Individual employees may be granted a maximum value of £250,000 per employee.
- The overall company limit is £3m.
- The company must be independent with less than 250 employees.
- The gross net asset value must be less than £30m.
- It has a potential tax rate of 10%.

SIP (Share Incentive Plan)

A SIP is an all-employee share plan which provides statutory tax relief for employees directly acquiring shares in a company.

Shares must be offered to all employees and be held in a trust. There will be no tax to pay if the shares are held for five years.

Employees can obtain shares in three ways:

Purchase: They may purchase shares out of their gross pay, with full income tax relief, limited to £1,800.

Free: Employees may be allocated free shares without paying income tax or National Insurance on their value, limited to £3,600.

Matching: Employees may be allocated up to two free Matching Shares for every share purchased, limited to £3,600.

The SIP creates employee shareholders where the risks and rewards for your employees are very similar to other shareholders.

Key Elements:
- Shares are held on behalf of employees in a trust.
- It is very flexible as to how shares are offered.
- It must be available to all employees.
- This is a long-term plan.

CSOP (Company Share Option Plan)

The CSOP is a tax qualified discretionary option plan under which a company may grant options to any employee or full-time director to acquire shares at fair market value, which can be agreed with HMRC before the grant.

Options can be awarded over the shares of UK private or listed companies and each employee can be granted options to buy shares with a maximum value of £30,000 at the date of the grant.

Key Elements:
- It has an individual limit of £30,000.
- This can be offered to all or some employees.
- It is suitable for any independent company, irrespective of size or sector.
- It is tax efficient – if exercised more than three years after the grant.

> **NOTE:** The figures and percentages mentioned above will change over time so please ensure you have the latest information from HMRC and other tax or regulatory bodies before proceeding.

In this section, we have looked at how an owner can exit their business using either external or internal options. The option that an owner chooses will depend on how quickly they need to exit the business, the tax advantages available to them and the type of legacy they wish to leave behind.

These decisions will require a lot of consideration and advice and should not be rushed. It is advisable to take your time, gather all the information and look at all the possible options available. Consider scenarios such as a change in personal circumstances – be it death, disease or disability, etc. Understand the tax implications and what type of legacy you want to leave.

Although there are pros and cons for all these options, the aim is to have an idea of which option you would like to target years before you expect to exit. Your target group may be very narrow, or you may want to target more than one group, which is fine. The main takeaway is that you – and the other directors/shareholders if applicable – need to be absolutely clear on who you are targeting and, in the interim, build your business accordingly.

Now that you have considered what type of exit or buyer you will be considering, you need to get your business ready for the exit process. This requires a fair bit of time to gather the necessary information and complete the preparations, and it will need to be updated annually. The sooner you start the process, the easier and better it will be for you when the time comes to exit your business.

Clarity Through a Value Assessment of Your Business

At the end of the business assessment, you will have a business attractiveness and business saleability score, each with a corresponding report. Each report will highlight areas that will require work or improvement to ensure both the attractiveness and saleability of the business are aligned. This will be measured on an annual basis.

Along with these two reports, you will know the value range of your business and how it is performing against other companies in your sector.

In this chapter, we have completed our examination of one leg of the three-legged stool, the business plan, in order for you to gain the Clarity needed to determine where your business is currently at. In the Value Assessment of your business 'leg', there are five main elements that we have considered and explored:

- Business attractiveness assessment: looking at your business from the outside
- Business saleability assessment: looking at your business from the inside
- Business valuation: transferable and financial valuations
- Business financial due diligence and benchmarking: business financial performance
- Buyer and exit analysis: ascertaining the best exit for you

Up to this point, you will have conducted a business attractiveness assessment, a business saleability assessment, a business valuation that focuses on both transferable and financial valuations, financial due diligence with industry benchmarking and have carried out an exit and buyer analysis to determine how you would like to exit your business and, if you are planning to sell, who your target buyer is likely to be.

As you'll soon learn in the Control and Consistency phases, you will assess these areas of your business on an annual basis. This is when you measure and track your progress over the previous 12 months and use those findings to plan for the next 12 months. In this way, you are strengthening your business as you get it ready for exit at a future date.

In upcoming chapters addressing the Control phase, I will show you how to take the results from these assessments and apply them to your business using the MAP (Master Action Plan). This is where we create a working plan to make key changes to your business for the coming 12 months. But for now, all we are doing is gathering information to gain Clarity on where your business is at in this moment in time – your location.

Once your business plan is completed, to finish the Clarity phase of the Business By Design methodology, we then need to move on to your personal plan and your financial plan, the other two legs of the stool. In much the same way, we gather information to gain Clarity on your current location from a personal and financial perspective, which is what we will explore in the following chapters.

Chapter 6 Takeaways

- A Value Assessment of your business, personal life and finances will enable you to gain Clarity over each area and give you the information you need to move each area forward.

- The business plan aspect of the Value Assessment is split into five elements:
  - Business attractiveness
  - Business saleability
  - Business valuation
  - Financial due diligence and benchmarking
  - Buyer and exit analysis

- You must not confuse attractiveness (what your business looks like from the outside) with saleability (what your business looks like from the inside).

- There are certain aspects of your business that you can assess and then work on to make sure that it is both attractive and saleable to a buyer.

- You must understand the difference between financial value and transferable value and work towards these values being the same.

- There are several methods that can be used to value a business. Different methods may be suited to different types and sizes of business, as well as to certain scenarios. It is helpful to use at least three different methods to achieve a balanced valuation.

- There are different ways to exit your business, with some being more suited to you depending on your type of business. It is important to have a plan early on for how you would exit so that you can work towards this model.

- There are different options for selling your business, and some may be more suited to your business and future plans than others. It is good to analyse the buyer types, weigh up the pros and cons if each type and have a clear idea of your preferred buyer type years before you expect to sell so that you can build and prepare your business accordingly for when the time comes to put it on the market.

- There are different types of deal structures, so it is useful to be aware of them and which one you would be prepared to work with should a buyer make an offer at a time you are ready to sell.

CHAPTER 7

Your Personal Plan

BEING A BUSINESS OWNER demands a lot. The stakes are high. As the business grows, the demand for our time increases. If we are not careful, we find ourselves working 10- to 15-hour days, coming home to eat and sleep, working or sleeping during the weekend and, before we know it, the years have flown by. We wrap our identity in the business and pay very little attention to all the other important parts of our lives. This will impact two main areas. The first is the outcome of the business sale, especially during the negotiation phase. And if – this is a big 'if' – the sale is successful, the effects will most certainly be felt post exit.

Many business owners view their business as an extension of themselves and, as such, they hold a skewed view of it. If a buyer appears to criticise their business, it feels like a personal insult (remember the ugly baby syndrome?). When this happens, emotions cloud judgement and the business owner cannot see things clearly. This is one of the primary reasons why deals collapse early on in the process: the business owner is too emotionally attached to their business.

The other factor that may affect us as business owners as we transition from our business to another opportunity (which could include retirement) is our emotional state. At some point post sale, we may start to feel regret, failure or lack of identity and purpose. These emotions will be more noticeable if other areas of our lives have been neglected in lieu of our sole focus on the business.

A survey of business owners shows that 75%
become dissatisfied with the result post exit.
—State of Owner Readiness Survey Report,
Exit Planning Institute (EPI), 2013.

As the above quote illustrates, three out of every four owners who sell their businesses become dissatisfied post exit; they get 'seller's remorse'. In other words, they sell their business and then, even if they received a good price and terms for their business, are disappointed with their life afterwards. Their life without their business.

Let's consider the following graph, showing the typical emotions that a seller may experience post exit.

Emotional turbulance following imposed change

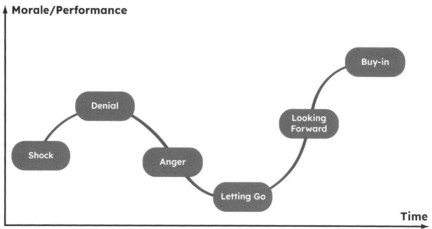

First researched by Elisabeth Kubler-Ross, Tavistock, 1969

The challenging emotions happen because the business owner did not consider what their life would look like once they exited their business. They had no plan, nothing to move on to. Many people, whether employed or an owner of their own business, cannot conceive of a life without a full work schedule, and when this suddenly happens, with unlimited space and time on their hands, they can feel aimless and unsettled. Being a business owner can be all-consuming with no time to develop hobbies and interests outside of work, or to contemplate what life will look like post exit.

During your time as a business owner, you will likely be working 40 to 70 hours a week, so you get used to constant busyness – responding to situations and problems, and always having something to do. Once you have exited your business, you are left to fill the 40- to 70-hour-a-week gap that is now in your life. You're no longer driven by the demands of others; what you do now is completely up to you. If you have made no plan to transition from business owner to ex-business owner, it could leave you with 'seller's remorse', which will raise its head in one of two scenarios:

1. A business owner is about to sell their business but, at the last minute, changes their mind, cancels the sale and takes the business off the market. This is not down to a bad offer or terms for the business, or even about the buyer. It is about the seller's emotional state towards the business. They have not planned for what life will be like post exit; they do not know what they will do to fill the void left by the sale of the business and they default to what they know and what they feel certain about.

2. The other scenario is where a business owner does sell the business but subsequently suffers real dissatisfaction because they do not know what to do next. Or they may think they sold the business for less than it is worth or maybe sold it at the wrong time.

These regrets creep in because for most business owners, their work contributes to their own sense of identity, as well as how they perceive others view them. They worry about their role within the family – what is their new status going to be? Some will worry about the employees they must leave behind and how the change in ownership may affect them and their lives.

According to an EPI survey from 2013, 48% of participants stated that they had 'no plans' post exit, and only 4% of participants had a formal written plan for their life after exit. Given these statistics, and the considerations for how business owners may respond to exiting their business without any plan for what their life will look like afterwards, it shows how important it is to have a plan, i.e., Clarity, for what you'll want to be doing once you exit your business, giving you the best chance of successfully starting the next chapter of your life.

We start this Value Assessment of your personal life in a similar vein to that of your business in that we need to ascertain how ready you are personally to exit your business. This part of the exit planning process, along with the financial plan, are almost always forgotten and, as described above, if neglected, could lead either to the business owner deciding not to sell or to problems arising further down the line once the business has been sold.

To overcome these obstacles, we need to adopt a Value Assessment with a holistic approach that covers not only your business, but also your personal and financial plans, which will need to be worked on alongside your business plan and given the same priority. Returning to the three-legged stool analogy, we need to ensure that each leg of the stool has equal attention in order to maintain balance. The Business By Design methodology gives the needed Clarity to ensure all three legs are given equal attention and are subsequently monitored at all times.

The 5 Fs

Being personally exit ready hinges around the 5 Fs: friends, family, faith, fitness and finance. We'll discuss the finance element in more detail later on under 'Your Finance Plan', but let's unpack the other Fs here ...

Friends

The 'friends' factor is about your relationships outside of your immediate family and away from the work environment. Almost everything a person achieves in their life and every moment of joy occurs because of the willing involvement of another human being. If you think about some of your greatest or most memorable moments, there was probably another human being involved in some way. Many of these moments do require someone else – a friend or someone you know. On a larger scale, friendships encompass our communities, societies and the people we serve through what we do in our business.

Goals that you may want to consider concerning friends include:
• Maintaining and nurturing your current friendship group.
• Keeping in touch with close friends at least once a fortnight (not just on social media!).
• Growing your friendship group by starting a new hobby or activity.

These things will help to create balance in your life, both in the present and later on when you exit, and will give you something to focus on other than work.

Family

Families can be a stable unit generating happiness and memories that last a lifetime. It is about taking stock of all the elements within a family unit.

If you have children, be the best parent you can possibly be.

If you have a partner, be the best spouse you can possibly be.

If you still have parents, be the best son or daughter you can possibly be.

Purposefully investing in these relationships will create a stable environment for both you and your family members. Again, this is stability that you'll enjoy both currently and later on when you exit. I do appreciate families can be tricky – I know this first-hand – and this area is a constant work in progress, as with every one of the 5 Fs.

Goals that you may want to consider are:
- Spending time every day interacting with your children
- Having 'date night' once a week with your partner
- When at home, spending less of your time on screens and doing more non-screen activities as a couple or as a family (You could implement a digital sabbath where one day a week no one in the family is on a screen.)

Faith

I am not necessarily talking about religion here. This applies to everyone, whether you're religious or not, as there is probably something you believe in. What I encourage you to do is simply to find a 20-minute slot each week, preferably in the evening, where you can be alone with no outside distractions and no digital devices. During this time allow yourself to focus on the person you want to become or on the business you want to have in the future. This allows you to reduce the physical noise level around you and in your head so you can focus on the bigger picture, on what really matters.

At times, you could even include listening to music or going for a walk in nature. I do not know if you have ever experienced this yourself, but for me, when I go on holiday, for example, and allow my brain to calm down and stop rushing at a million miles an hour, it tends to be then that great ideas pop into my head. So, treat these 20 minutes a week like taking a little mini-holiday and give yourself a chance to refocus, slow down and maybe come up with a few new ideas. This practice should bring much-needed calm and perspective, both in your present and as you continue to practise in future years. It should also continue to provide you with positivity post exit.

Goals that you may want to consider are:
• Scheduling time to be quiet once a week and allowing yourself to focus on what you want to achieve
• Continuing this practice throughout your time leading up to your exit, as well as post exit to continue your scheduled weekly thinking time.

Fitness

This deals with your overall health, fitness, relaxation and sleep. Physical fitness is a way of keeping yourself healthy and strong. By looking after your body through exercise, eating healthily and sleeping sufficiently, you'll be able to be in the best condition possible for the challenges ahead. For me, it is also a way to improve my self-discipline and reduce my stress levels. Obviously, maintaining a good fitness regime aids you both currently and in the future.

Goals concerning your fitness to consider include:
• Having a healthier or more balanced diet
• Starting an exercise programme
• Undertaking a daily cold water immersion or shower (believe me – it works!)
• Improving your sleep patterns
• Increasing your daily water intake
• And many more (just look at Instagram!)

Finance

Money can be seen as a measurable reference for your life. It is effectively the average of your time, skill, experience, persistence, wisdom and relationships. It brings stability to your family and allows you to be generous to other people, like your friends and community, helping them and enriching their lives.

Goals you may want to consider around your finances are:
- Decreasing outgoings and increasing savings
- Starting and maintaining a monthly budget
- Reducing time spent on non-profitable activities such as watching TV or scrolling social media.

Building a personal plan

An activity to get you started in building a personal plan is to list 10 things in each of the 5 Fs that you'll work on over the next 90 days. Make a list of the things you might plan to start doing, do more of or stop doing altogether. Once you have done this, you'll have a list of 50 areas in your personal life that you can work on at the same time as getting your business ready for exit.

Next we will take a look at several elements within the 5 Fs and determine your personal readiness score, which will establish how ready you are personally to exit your business.

Personal Readiness

To gain Clarity on how ready you are to exit your business, for each of the following key life areas, take some time to articulate where you are at currently and where you'd like to be in the future:
- Achievement
- Business
- Character
- Emotional state
- Exit preparation
- Fun and recreation

- Health and fitness
- Intellectual development
- Life vision
- Love relationship
- Personal blocks
- Post-exit plans
- Quality of life
- Social life

Achievement

As business owners, we constantly set goals, work towards goals and achieve goals. It is something we do instinctively, and we evaluate ourselves against these goal achievements. However, it is vitally important that, along with our business goals, we do not forget our other aspirations outside of our working environment.

Life achievements can take many forms. You may have several goals or accomplishments that you wish to achieve, such as:

- Personal goals
- Financial goals
- Friends or family goals
- Sporting goals
- Charity goals

What goals do you have for your life?

It is important to regularly take a step back in order to align, or realign, the goals in all areas of our lives. We need to ensure that we have an emotional connection with each goal as well as a deadline for when we plan to achieve them. Our business should act as an enabler or facilitator to help achieve our goals rather than an inhibitor or an excuse as to why we do not accomplish them.

Business

Owning a business can be a huge time commitment and the context in which we spend most of our days. An element of this is the relationships and friendships that are formed within the business as well as with our clients and suppliers. Having good, healthy relationships, both inside and outside of our business, will have a big impact on our personal happiness, fulfilment and health, both currently and after we exit our business.

Does your business, and the work you do within it, fulfil you? Do you feel secure and confident in what you have built and the sector in which you operate?

It is worth taking some time to think about your role within the business and to consider whether you are satisfied with the work that you are doing.

Character

Our character is who we are when no one is looking. It includes all our personal and moral values, and our contribution to the community in which we live.

Does what you stand for come through in your business? Do you live your life in accordance with your set of standards and values?

Again, it is worth taking some time out to consider this: Is your business forming your character, or is your character forming the business?

Emotional State

Your emotional connection or 'tie' with your business is critical to ensuring a successful exit. Many owners are so emotionally invested in their business that it becomes their 'baby', and that can be a very risky position to hold. In that situation, the owner is unable to view their business objectively, potentially causing them to reject a perfectly good deal.

To overcome this problem, find areas outside of your business that you can start to focus on today, hopefully long before you exit. This will help to shift your identity and emotional attachment from your business to something else, thus benefiting you in the here and now and post exit.

Exit Preparation

On a scale of zero to ten, with zero equalling 'not at all' and ten equalling 'totally', how exit ready are you, your business and your finances? And how aware are you of the exit process and the need to prepare for it well in advance? Exit preparation is key to a successful exit. Take the time to evaluate your level of Clarity around the exit process and what happens during each phase. It is important to know and understand all your options and be able to make informed and rational decisions.

Fun and Recreation

This is all about creating balance in your life outside of your business.

Consider taking up a sport or hobby or learning a new skill – something that enables you to engage with people and helps you to feel part of something bigger than yourself. These activities will not only help you to extend your friendship circle but, will also improve your physical health and mental wellbeing. The people you meet and build friendships with will also enrich your life and give you a sense of purpose.

These activities will help to reduce stress, create balance within your life, and will start to prepare you for your post-exit life. Finding time for yourself and creating this balance will also improve your business before you exit. It allows for you to mentally recharge and, most of the time, will give you the thinking space or incidental conversations needed to find solutions or provide new ideas to drive your business forward. So, this process becomes a win-win.

Health and Fitness

This is closely linked with fun and recreation by addressing two key areas – your mental wellbeing and your physical wellbeing.

Mental Wellbeing

There are generally two aspects to improving our mental wellbeing. The first is to reduce stress. We cannot constantly live our life at 100 miles per hour. We need to allow ourselves to slow down and shift gears. In doing so, we allow our mind to recover, which will improve the Clarity and vision needed to make good decisions, both in our personal life and business life.

The second aspect of mental wellbeing is to stretch our mind and keep it active by learning something new or by looking for a fresh challenge. This will not only improve our mental fitness, but will also provide a sense of progress and achievement through meeting personal goals and improving our self-confidence.

Physical Wellbeing

Your physical wellbeing directly affects every other area of your life. Therefore, it is vital to make this a priority, especially as this will have a far-reaching impact in later life, post exit.

We need to ensure that we have a regular exercise routine, eat a balanced diet, drink enough water and have sufficient, high-quality sleep. Getting this right will impact our mood and energy levels throughout the day and will grant us better decision-making abilities, leading to better outcomes.

Intellectual Development

Your intellectual development can be both business related and personal. Each contributes to your overall intellectual progress.

Identify areas in your life that you want to develop and set yourself quarterly or yearly goals, either to improve those areas or to gain new skills. This could include reading, or listening to, personal development books, attending related courses or developing new healthy habits.

The key is to never stop learning, growing and improving. It needs to be intentional and is something that will require focus and deliberate action.

Life Vision

What is your life vision? Have you ever stopped to think about it?

Knowing your purpose as an individual, as well as the purpose of your business, will give you the Clarity and certainty as to why you are doing what you do. By knowing where you are heading, you can measure your progress.

So, by knowing who you are personally, along with the reason for your business and the impact you want to have on this world, you can make every day intentional and seek to make a positive difference for those around you.

Love Relationship

Your relationship with your partner will impact all areas of your life. Being in a bad relationship can be draining and will cause you to lose focus and drive. It is therefore important to look at the health of that relationship and how it can be nurtured and improved.

A book that I highly recommend is *The Five Love Languages* by Gary Chapman. It gives a wonderful insight into relationships and how individuals both give and receive love.

As with all other aspects of our personal life, giving attention to and nurturing our love relationship can empower and energise every part of our life, both business and personal. If this area of your life has been neglected in favour of your business, I would strongly advise you take a look at this so that you have a love relationship that survives the journey to life post exit.

Personal Blocks

As countless business coaches will attest to, our mindset can be one of the biggest barriers to our success. The challenge is to unearth exactly what holds you back from a happier and more successful life, and then to implement practical and realistic steps to overcome these barriers and become more confident, courageous and capable of pursuing the direction of your dreams.

The areas we need to assess include self-confidence, self-discipline, time management, procrastination levels, our skills and focus as a leader and manager and our ability to build relationships and set boundaries. Listed below are the most common areas where personal blocks can exist, but this is not an exhaustive list. Take some time out to think about your own mindset and possible barriers.

- Self-doubt or fear
- Self-confidence
- Procrastination
- Perseverance
- Poor self-image
- Perfectionism
- Self-discipline
- Assertiveness

Post-Exit Plans

The key to a successful post-exit life is having a deep understanding of your financial situation. This will vary from person to person, depending on age, financial assets, lifestyle, etc., so this will need to be a plan tailored for you. You will need to find out 'Your Number', the amount of money you will need upon retirement in order to live the lifestyle you want, without the fear of ever running out of money (we address how to find Your Number in chapter 8).

A post-exit plan also considers what would happen should you be forced to exit your business earlier than anticipated. This could be due to ill health, injury, death, or a change in your personal circumstances. Being prepared for the worst-case scenario will provide you with the options and the means to deal with any unexpected future events.

Quality of Life

This has to do with your environment and how satisfied you are with your surroundings, which is very important because being content and well organised will improve your overall performance and focus. It will set you up to operate more efficiently and, ultimately, to achieve more.

On the other hand, living in an environment that is cluttered or where you feel unhappy will cause your focus to shift, leading you to become less motivated and less productive. This is especially true if that environment is your business because it is highly possible that, if you are feeling like that, so are your staff.

Social Life

We all have areas of influence that radiate from us. Our impact has a ripple effect. It is greatest with our immediate family and close friends and then gets weaker as it moves further away. Therefore, it is prudent to choose wisely with whom you spend your time as those choices will have the greatest impact on your future. Where you will be in five- or 10-years' time will be influenced by those people.

Surround yourself with people who will push you in every area of your life, with people who are better than you and who will encourage you. This will have a profound impact on your mental, physical and emotional wellbeing.

Perhaps in this personal Value Assessment, you've been asked about issues or areas of your life that you may have never considered before, and it may be difficult to respond immediately. That is perfectly normal because, after all, most of your time has been focused on your business and other such important elements. As a result, considering these other areas of your life and gaining Clarity in these areas may feel alien for a lot of business owners, at least at first, but take your time and consider each aspect one by one.

It is worth remembering that planning for life post exit does not begin the day after you have exited your business. Planning and putting measures in place needs to start several years before exiting. It is essential to start carving out time from your busy work schedule, to start to change old habits or mindsets, and to start planning what your life will look like after you exit your business today, rather than waiting until after you've exited.

To help with this process I would encourage you to think about and write down the following:

- If you could do anything other than work in your business, what would it be?
- Have you any hobbies or goals you would like to pursue? Who do you do these with?
- What did you enjoy doing before you had your business? Who did you do this with?
- What is stopping or preventing you from pursuing these activities now?
- What do you currently do outside of work? Who do you do it with?

Starting to think about your life in this way will help focus your attention on your life and the people around you. It is the first step to gaining Clarity and becoming personally ready for a life post exit.

Before moving on to gaining Clarity around your financial plan, the subject of the next chapter, I would like to leave you with this poem:

What Will Matter
by Michael Josephson

Ready or not, some day it will all come to an end.

There will be no more sunrises, no minutes, hours, or days.

All the things you collected, whether treasured or forgotten, will pass to someone else.

Your wealth, fame, and temporal power will shrivel to irrelevance.

It won't matter what you owned or what you were owed.

Your grudges, resentments, frustrations, and jealousies will finally disappear.

So, too, your hopes, ambitions, plans and to-do lists will expire.

The wins and losses that once seemed so important will fade away.

It won't matter where you came from or what side of the tracks you lived on at the end.

It won't matter whether you were beautiful or brilliant.

Even your gender and skin colour will be irrelevant.

So what will matter?

How will the value of your days be measured?

What will matter is not what you bought but what you built; not what you got but what you gave.

What will matter is not your success but your significance.

What will matter is not what you learned but what you taught.

What will matter is every act of integrity, compassion, courage, or sacrifice that enriched, empowered, or encouraged others to emulate your example. What will matter is not your competence but your character.

What will matter is not how many people you knew but how many will feel a lasting loss when you're gone.

What will matter is not your memories but the memories that live in those who loved you.

What will matter is how long you'll be remembered, by whom, and for what.

Living a life that matters doesn't happen by accident.

It's not a matter of circumstance but of choice.

Choose to live a life that matters.

Chapter 7 Takeaways

- When ascertaining your current situation and planning your exit, it is important to not only focus on your business plan, but also on your personal and financial plans.

- As with your business plan, you need to develop your personal plan for your current life and your post-exit life years before you intend to exit your business.

- Business owners are often so caught up in running and working in their business that they leave little or no time to develop hobbies, interests and relationships outside of work.

- After exiting, many business owners experience 'seller's remorse'.

- Being personally exit ready hinges around the 5 Fs: friends, family, faith, fitness and finance.

- You can build a personal plan of things you want to start doing, do more of or stop doing altogether.

- To gain Clarity on your personal exit readiness, you can consider a number of key life areas to ascertain where you are now and where you would like to be in the future:
  - Achievement
  - Business
  - Character
  - Emotional state
  - Exit preparation
  - Fun and recreation
  - Health and fitness
  - Intellectual development
  - Life vision
  - Love relationship
  - Personal blocks
  - Post-exit plans
  - Quality of life
  - Social life

CHAPTER 8

Your Financial Plan

UP TO THIS POINT, we've looked at how to gain Clarity through a Value Assessment of your business and your personal life – the first two legs of the stool. In this chapter, we arrive at the third leg of our three-legged stool: your finances.

What is your financial plan for your future? What are you aiming for? What does it look like, and how would you know if you have achieved it? What is 'Your Number' – the amount of money you will need to live on for the rest of your life after you exit your business?

These are questions we have probably all asked ourselves but, in all honesty, have you really thought about it? I know there was a time when I had not. I had a vague idea of what I wanted and knew the general direction I needed to go in, but there was no detail and no Clarity. In truth, I do not think I would even have known whether or not I had achieved what I thought I had set out to!

Not knowing what Your Number is could result in one of two outcomes:

Outcome 1: You think you know what your destination is, but when you actually get there, you discover it is the wrong place. This is the situation in which many business owners find themselves. They have an idea in their head of how much they will need to retire on and are relying on the sale of their business to bridge the gap between where they currently think they are and where they need to be to retire comfortably. Most business owners have their wealth tied up in their business, but what if the business is not worth what they think it is?

What will happen if they are forced to exit the business earlier than planned but cannot close the wealth gap in time? There won't be the time to rectify it, and this could put them in a terrible financial predicament.

Outcome 2: Some business owners have the opposite problem, a truly fortunate but equally sad position. They think they need far more than what they really do. For example, a business owner may think they need to sell the business for £5m to achieve financial security, when in fact all they need is £2m. So they end up working for many more years than they really needed to, when in reality they could have exited their business years earlier and enjoyed the life they were dreaming of and working towards.

Both outcomes stem from not knowing Your Number and not taking a holistic approach to developing and growing your business plan, personal plan and financial plan.

How do you figure out what you need financially and translate this back into both your personal and business plans? Let's look at that in this chapter.

Your Number

Like for any journey, you need to know your destination. You need this Clarity. For your journey towards exit, you need to know Your Number.

Your Number is the amount of money you will need upon retirement to live on for the rest of your life, maintaining the lifestyle you want, without the fear of ever running out of money. This could include holidaying every year, paying for weddings, buying a holiday home, helping your children get onto the property ladder, leaving a legacy for your grandchildren, etc. Your Number should enable you to provide for your family and allow you to live the lifestyle that is comfortable and financially secure – without the fear of ever running out of money.

There is some great software out there that wealth planners can use to calculate what Your Number will need to be. The software can go into great detail and assess thousands of options, possibilities and scenarios. Once this number has been calculated by a wealth planner, they will assess where you are currently from a financial perspective against the number they have calculated. In most cases, there is a gap, called the wealth gap. The wealth gap is the difference between where you are currently and where you want to be in the future. This gap may be large or it may be small, but the key is knowing that there is a gap. As the future is uncertain, it would be wise to speak with your wealth planner and put into place various insurance policies to cover that wealth gap, just in case of injury, illness, disability, or death. In doing so, you will be covered if something unforeseen were to happen.

Your wealth planner can then create a personal investment plan to help bridge the wealth gap, working closely with your business advisor. Your business advisor's role is to help you to develop your business so that it will help to bridge the gap, which is achieved by creating a business plan, as detailed in chapter 6.

It will be the role of the business advisor and the wealth planner to regularly assess this wealth gap and to ensure you as the business owner are always prepared for exit. As soon as that wealth gap has been closed and you have reached your financial destination – Your Number – then you can pull the trigger and set things in motion to exit your business.

Your Financial Plan

Determining Your Number is just the start of making your financial plan. The other areas that your financial plan will cover include:

- Business value and personal wealth
- Debt management
- Estate and tax planning
- Personal finances
- Personal wealth planner
- Risk management: The 5 Ds
- Tax and investment strategies
- Wealth management

We look at each of these areas in turn throughout the rest of this chapter.

Business Value and Personal Wealth

According to *The Exit Planning Institute (EPI)*, between 80% and 90% of an owner's wealth is tied up in their business, and yet:

- Two-thirds of business owners do not know all their exit options.
- 78% have no transition plan.
- 83% have no written plan.
- 49% have no plan at all.
- 40% have not planned for any unexpected events.
- 86% have not carried out a strategic review or value assessment growth plan.

Many business owners do not know Their Number. Obtaining this critical information, as well as the current value of your business, is paramount to you knowing what needs to be done to achieve your goals. You must get Clarity on these numbers in order to plan for and enact the best exit possible. Ideally this should be reviewed at least once a year.

Debt Management

Debt and the use of external finances can be vital in growing a business. This includes any personal, director, commercial, or personal guaranteed loans, or credit card debt used to generate capital in order to expand and grow a business.

Before taking on any debt, it is imperative to create a cash flow forecast to ensure the debt can be serviced and set out a plan of how and when the loans will be paid back. Keeping on top of this and securing the best possible deal will make for cheaper borrowing and better control over your cash flow.

Estate and Tax Planning

Making your money work hard for you and having a personal investment strategy is part of the exit planning process. Ideally, this work should be carried out by a respected wealth planner who can look at your whole situation and involve your business advisor and/or your accountant to ensure everything is on track and make adjustments if necessary.

Gaining Clarity about your personal financial landscape will feed into your business strategy, allowing you and your advisors to make the most informed decisions possible. Forewarned is forearmed!

Personal Finances

This is tightly linked to estate and tax planning as being part of the three-legged stool. This is where you assess your current financial position and determine where you would like to be at some point in the future.

Carrying out a personal monthly budget with a cash flow statement and net worth tracking sheet is a great way of keeping track of your personal financial journey. Having real-time, updated information will allow you to make the most informed decisions possible.

Personal Wealth Planner

Support with your personal estate and finances needs to be done by a professional with a proven track record. It will be their job to look after your overall personal wealth and to create a personal investment plan for you that will meet your needs. This plan will need to be reviewed on an annual basis and will need to include communication with your business advisor or accountant. Together with you, they will ensure all the legs of your three-legged stool are given equal attention to create balance within your portfolio.

Risk Management: The 5 Ds

We all know life can be unpredictable, and that is why being prepared will give you the best chance possible to exit your business successfully.

The dreaded 5 Ds are:
- Distress
- Disagreement
- Disease/Disability
- Divorce
- Death

Your business advisor or accountant will work with you to de-risk the potential negative impact of these events by firstly assessing what you currently have in place and then considering what you may need going forward. As with your wealth planner, these processes should be reviewed annually.

Tax and Investment Strategies

As part of working with a wealth planner, you should receive regular updates as to how your portfolio is doing. This will allow you to work together to ensure your money is working hard for you and then make any changes during your annual review.

Wealth Management

For business owners who have most of their wealth tied to their business, it is important to grow this asset as much as possible.

As already discussed, the biggest reason for a reduced business valuation is owner reliance, where the business is too reliant upon its owner. Due to the risks involved, owner reliance will cause a buyer to reduce what they are prepared to pay for a business. The best way to overcome this is to make yourself redundant within the operational side of your business. Replace yourself with people whose specific role it will be to take care of the day-to-day running of the business.

As part of this plan, the business must also fund your financial plan by taking money out of the business as tax efficiently as possible to help close the wealth gap. The ideal scenario would be to close the wealth gap without the need to sell your business. That way you will not be at the mercy of market trends or forces beyond your control and the sale of your business will be a bonus.

Business, Personal and Financial Clarity: Currently and Your Vision for the Future

From chapter 5 to chapter 8, we have discussed all three legs of the three-legged stool – your business plan, your personal plan and your financial plan. Carrying out Value Assessments in these three areas will give you Clarity you need to allow you to get a very accurate idea of where you are at – in other words, your current location. This is the vital first step in creating an exit strategy.

Alongside this first step, you will start to focus on where you want to ultimately end up – your destination. Through the Value Assessment, you will know what your business needs to be worth, what you need to do from a personal perspective to become exit ready and how much money you will need in order to achieve the financial freedom you want.

However, at this stage, you might not know what you want your final destination to look like. An unclear final destination is not uncommon, but it is important to start creating a picture of what that destination might look like for you. Over time, the exact details of that destination may evolve and change but it is important to start off with a vision rather than no idea of what you are working towards. From a practical point of view, as mentioned previously, if you don't have a destination in mind, how will you know whether you have reached your goal and when it is the right time to exit your business? (Remember those business owners with no goal in mind who either had to work for longer than they had intended or worked for longer than necessary because they didn't realise they had reached their retirement goal.)

From a personal perspective, it is so important to create a clear vision for your future. Even though it might seem early to plan your future years ahead, this is vital because, as you go through the Stabilise-Systemise-Scale Process, there will be times when your life and/or your business gets tough, when you feel as if developing your business and getting it exit ready is a process that will never end. You may even question why you are even working through this process in the first place. Having a strong vision already in place will help you to remain focused and persistent and will give you the motivation you need to keep going until you ultimately execute all the aspects of the Stabilise-Systemise-Scale Process and enjoy an optimal exit.

So, in the next chapter we will look at your vision and start to add colour and emotion to what your future will look like so that you can clearly see, feel and know your particular destination. This will be a personal vision for your future. No one else can create this for you as it is so personal, but I will guide you through the steps for you to begin to create your very own vision.

Chapter 8 Takeaways

- To be able to build a financial plan, you need to know Your Number – the amount of money you will need upon retirement in order to live the lifestyle you want without fear of ever running out of money.

- Not knowing Your Number could result in you working for longer than you intend or longer than you need.

- Once you have determined Your Number, you can calculate the wealth gap between your current financial position and the finances you require to exit your business and work with your wealth planner and business advisor to bridge this gap.

- You can work with your accountant and business advisor to de-risk your business from the potential negative impact of any of the 5 Ds.

- Once you have Clarity in all three areas – business, personal and financial – you can begin to create a vision for your future destination.

CHAPTER 9

Your Vision

WE HAVE NOW ADDRESSED your business, personal and financial plans. This has enabled us to achieve the Clarity necessary for determining where you currently are on your map of life. It is now time to determine where you want to end up – your ultimate destination.

The purpose of having a vision, be it five, 10, 15, or even 20 years down the line, is to have a tangible objective to work towards so that you can put plans in place within your business that will steer you towards your goals. Creating a vision for your future will help you to calculate Your Number as your vision will determine the amount of money you will need to be able to exit, and by knowing Your Number, you are better placed to create a strategic plan that develops your business towards this. By creating a vivid picture of what that life will look like for you – something visual and meaningful – you are establishing an end goal, which will help you to remain focused and motivated when the journey is feeling tough.

To begin to establish your vision, you now need to ask yourself what you envisage your business, your personal life and your financial position to be like by the point at which you wish to exit your business.

Over the following sections, take some time to imagine what each of these three legs of the stool might look like for you – try to be as detailed as you can!

Business Vision

What do you want your business to look like at the point in time when you wish to exit? It is worth taking the time to carefully consider what you really want your company to be like.

Visualise things like:

- How many employees will you have? How many people will be on your management team?
- What is your company's structure? Create an organisational chart for your employees.
- Who will be your trusted advisors? Your exit advisor, wealth planner and tax and estate advisor?
- What will it feel to be your company's CEO? Try to imagine yourself in this role and describe how you feel.
- How many weeks' holiday will you be able to take over the course of a year?
- What culture do you want your business to have?
- What will your premises look like? Where will it be?
- Will you have several branches or offices? How will these be organised and managed?
- Picture yourself walking into your office. What will that look and feel like?
- How much profit will your business need to be making to achieve your financial goals?
- How will you feel knowing that you and your business are prepared for whatever life may throw at you? What difference will that make to you and your family?

These are just a few examples of the level of detail you want to envision concerning your business at the point of exit. By creating this clear, detailed vision, you will establish tangible goals that can be worked towards and specific features that will be put in place along the journey.

Personal Vision

What will your personal life look like at the point you plan to exit your business? As discussed in chapter 7, as business owners, we are often all-consumed by our work, leaving little or no time to develop our lives outside of the business. By establishing a vision for your personal life, you will not only have exciting plans to look forward to when you do exit your business, but also, as you begin to withdraw from the day-to-day running of the business towards becoming your company's CEO, there will start to be time for you to develop your personal life whilst you are still working, so some of the activities in your personal vision could start sooner than your actual exit. As with your business, take some time to imagine what your ideal personal life could look like once you exit.

- What hobbies, activities or sports will you be doing?
- What holidays will you plan?
- What will you have accomplished by that time?
- If you are still going to be working at that point, how many hours per week/month will that be?
- What community or outreach projects will you be involved in?
- How do you envisage your relationships, both inside and outside of your business?
- How will you feel the day after you exit the business? What will you put in place to help your transition?

This is not an exhaustive list; you may have other aspects of life outside of work that you see yourself starting, developing and becoming involved in, both in the lead-up to your exit and afterwards. Your vision may also evolve along your journey, in response to the ebb and flow of life, but it is better to have a vision and adapt it than to have no vision and therefore no direction of travel or plan for your life once your time is your own.

Financial Vision

Implementing a personal investment strategy is vital to ensuring you are able to retire with enough money in order to live the lifestyle you want, without the fear of running out of money. What would achieving that future financial goal mean for you and your family? Create a picture in your mind of what that would look like and what it will allow you to do.

- What sort of legacy do you want to leave for your children and grandchildren?
- What tax strategies have you employed so that you are as tax efficient as possible?
- What healthcare plan have you got in place?
- Do you have a dream car you want to buy?
- Will you buy a holiday home somewhere?
- What is your net worth?
- Who is your wealth planner?

It is critical that you connect on an emotional level with what you see in your business, personal and financial vision. This means that you not only visualise what your future will look like, but also how you will be feeling when you achieve this amazing milestone. Combining your vision with the emotions you will be feeling will help to make your vision a reality. It will also help to sustain you during the times where the journey is hard, when you are working all the hours God sends and it feels as if the exhausting work will never end. When you feel like this, you can take a step back, return to your vision and reconnect with 'your why' – the reason why you are investing your time, energy and effort. Having a strong vision will provide you with needed grounding and will motivate you to keep on going. I would encourage you to spend a good amount of time on this section and become very clear of what the future will look like for you. You may wish to create a vision board or vision book to have something really visual to refer to, or you may share your visions with your family and/or close work colleagues so that your own vision becomes a shared vision for your business and your family. However you choose to document your vision, get it really clear so that when times get tough, you can quickly recall why you're doing what you're doing.

You have now completed the Clarity part of the process that uses the Value Assessment to measure and gauge what the three legs of your stool look like:

Clarity—Your Business Plan: Here we focused on gaining clarity in terms of your business attractiveness, saleability, valuation, financial due diligence, benchmarking and exit and buyer analysis. Business attractiveness looks at what your business looks like from the outside, and business saleability looks at what your business looks like from the inside. We found that both need to line up to achieve a successful exit.

Clarity—Your Personal Plan: This is an often-neglected area of a business owner's life which involves consciously thinking about your life post exit and then building or creating a life to which you can transition once you leave your business.

Clarity—Your Financial Plan: This allows you to know for definite how much money you need to retire and live the lifestyle you want without the fear of ever running out of money.

This brings to a close the first step in the Stabilise-Systemise-Scale Process – Clarity – where we use the Value Assessment to determine exactly where you are, your location, and where you want to be – your destination. It is designed to help determine your starting point from three key perspectives: business, personal and financial. Then, using your vision, you create a focus, a destination point that you will work towards.

With these two points in place, we can move on to the next step in the process: Control. This is where we join the dots, where we create a roadmap to plan your journey from where you are now to where you want to be in the future.

Chapter 9 Takeaways

- It is important to have a vision for your business, your personal life and your finances at the point of your exit so that you have tangible goals to plan for and work towards.

- Having a clear vision for your future will keep you motivated when the journey gets tough.

- You need to take time to consider a detailed picture of your business, your personal life and your finances at the point of your exit and how this will feel for you, your family and your colleagues.

- Creating your vision will take time and you may find that your visions change and evolve over time, but it is better to have a flexible vision than no vision at all.

- As you withdraw from the day-to-day running of your business and become your company's CEO, you should find that you have more time available to pursue interests and hobbies outside of work, so some of your personal visions may begin during your journey towards exit.

- Creating a vision board/book or sharing your visions with your family and colleagues may document and cement your visions for you as well as get others on board with your journey.

- Once you have ascertained your current location and end destination, you can move to the next phase – Control – where you begin to plan a route between the two.

PHASE 2: CONTROL
CHAPTER 10
Value Pathway

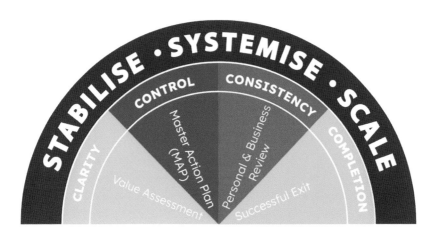

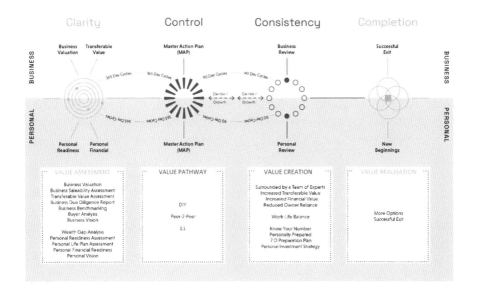

IN CHAPTERS 5 TO 9, we looked at the first part of the Stabilise-Systemise-Scale Process, which is Clarity. Once we have Clarity, we are in the position to gain Control. Beforehand, for most business owners, their situation controls them but as soon as we are clear about where we are and where we're going, we can reverse this situation and place ourselves in control. By knowing your objectives, creating a plan towards them and working on your plan in a very systematic and focused way, you immediately gain more Control. The more Control you gain and the more action you take, the closer you'll get to your goals and objectives – to successfully exit your business when required.

As already discussed, to gain this Clarity, we need to undertake a Value Assessment of the three key areas – business, personal and financial – which has been designed in such a way as to create a holistic picture of your business, personal and financial plans. This will give you a good understanding of where you and your business are right now. We'll also know your destination – your end goal – from a business, personal and financial perspective. Therefore with these two points in place, we can start to create a pathway to bridge the gap between where you are now and where you want to be.

Value Pathway: Your MAP

Within the Control phase of the Stabilise-Systemise-Scale Process lies the Value Pathway. At this point, you choose how you will journey this pathway from your starting point to your destination. This entire methodology is designed to provide you with many options for how you work through it because when you have the power to choose, you have Control. From the results of your Value Assessment under the Clarity Phase, you will create a Master Action Plan (MAP) of the actions, changes and developments that you will work on in your business, personal and financial plans in order to work towards your goals.

As every owner is different, how you navigate this part of the journey (the Value Pathway) is flexible; you can choose which of the three routes will work best for you.

1. *Do-It-Yourself (DIY):* At this stage, you have all the information you need to get you to your destination. All you have to do is work on the MAP, focusing on all the de-risking and growth activities, all of which will be highlighted in your Master Action Plan.

2. *Join a Peer-to-Peer Group:* Some business owners prefer to undertake this journey with other like-minded entrepreneurs. There is security in being part of a group of people undertaking the same journey. There is strength in numbers, and if one owner is struggling, the resources and input of the group can help them to move forward.

3. *One-to-One:* For those owners who would like to take a more accelerated approach, there is a one-to-one option. Whilst an intense experience, you will cover a lot more ground, using the team and resources of an approved advisor.

At Business By Design, our team of approved advisors and other experts would be delighted to partner with you to support you on your journey, whether 1:1 or part of a group. If either of these is your preferred route, contact us at **hello@businessbydesign.co.uk** to find out more.

To gain Control, you start by implementing your Master Action Plan (MAP). A Master Action Plan is a list created from the findings of your Value Assessment. It's a list of all the areas within your business, personal and financial plans that will need to be addressed to help get you to your destination, your vision and your exit. Think of this list as a set of waypoints to help guide you step by step towards your end goal. You will select a number of tasks to work on within your business and to work on personally within a given time period, which I recommend being 90 days. In each 90-day cycle, I would suggest working on no more than five tasks from your business plan and five tasks from across your personal and financial plans (ten tasks in total). At the end of every 90 days, you will review your progress and replace completed tasks with further actions from your MAP. As tasks are completed, you'll begin to see growth and value being added to your business and you should see an improvement in your personal life as you gain more control of your business, moving towards being its CEO and releasing your time for family, friends and other interests. In the long term, the impact of your MAP work will be tracked and measured by annually working through the Value Assessment.

The Master Action Plan (MAP) will highlight all the areas that need to be worked on throughout your journey from your starting point to your destination. At first, this may seem daunting and overwhelming. In the initial stages of your journey, these tasks will have implications on your already depleted time and financial resources which, for some business owners, could cause a fight, flight or freeze response. Whatever you may feel and whatever your usual reaction would be to this type of situation, I want to encourage you to resist the urge to either take a 'scattergun' approach to the list (addressing various problem areas randomly and inconsistently) or to take the 'ostrich' approach (hide the list away and put your head in the sand). These approaches generally lead to discouragement and frustration, and they certainly don't lead to you preparing a viable exit strategy. Instead, there's a strategic way to sequence your MAP tasks in order to get the most impact for your efforts. Following that sequence will give structure to your journey and minimise your feelings of overwhelm or discouragement.

As outlined in this chapter, the Stabilise-Systemise-Scale Process has a structured method that ensures you carry out these tasks in a certain order, an order that will allow you to protect the wealth you have already created, provide a stable platform for growth and create the resources you need to grow and develop your three plans. This process creates a rhythm for you and your company, but as with anything new, it will require you to take action, be disciplined and lead from the front.

Remember this is not a sprint but a marathon and, as such, will need to be broken down into bite-sized chunks and short-term goals. That is why we use the 90-day cycles. Each 90-day cycle is extremely focused and the method of setting, working through and reviewing a manageable set of tasks every 90 days is designed to give you the very best chance of success. This chapter addresses all of these factors.

So, if you're ready for the challenge, let us begin!

Implementing the Master Action Plan (MAP)

The Value Assessment you completed in the Clarity phase focuses on the three legs of your stool – your business, personal and financial plans. It reveals which areas are strong and which areas will require some work.

During the Value Assessment, you considered each leg of the stool in myriad facets through responding to multiple questions for each aspect. At Business By Design, we have developed software that will take your responses to each of the areas, process your answers and produce a report that sequences these areas, ranking them from your worst- to your best-performing so that you are able to strategically sequence and prioritise tasks. This list of tasks becomes your Master Action Plan (MAP) from which you'll select a manageable set of tasks for each 90-day cycle, enabling you to realistically scale your business and increase its value, as well as address any areas in your personal or financial life that may be at risk or require some attention.

If you would like to use the Business By Design Value Assessment tool to process and rank your responses and create your sequenced MAP, we would be pleased to work with you. Contact us at **hello@businessbydesign.co.uk** to find out more. Alternatively, you can undertake a free mini Value Assessment and receive a free mini MAP (Master Action Plan) by visiting: **www.thesmarterexit.com**

Remember: When it comes to tackling the tasks, like with any journey, it will require focus, determination and consistently moving step by step towards your end destination. Many business owners are aware of what needs to be done but are either too busy to tackle the required tasks or are intimidated and overwhelmed by the sheer volume of what needs to be done. To overcome these obstacles and to start making progress, you need to implement a strategy that focuses only on a handful of tasks at a time. In their book *The One Thing*, authors Gary Keller and Jay Papasan talk about the importance of focus and cultivating better habits. They go on to explain that although many people feel as if they achieve more when multitasking, it is actually an unfruitful approach because success requires long periods of laser-like concentration, not scattershot swats, which is what I mentioned earlier as the 'scattergun' approach, one that I discourage anyone from practising as it simply isn't an effective method. As already mentioned, I recommend no more than ten tasks from across your business, personal and financial plans to work on per 90-day cycle.

Categorising the Tasks: De-Risking or Growth

The list of tasks that you will need to work on to become exit ready should not be addressed in a random, scattergun way. Instead, a strategic approach is necessary, where you determine which tasks make the most sense to tackle first, then which to tackle next, and then which to do after that. At first, your list may contain dozens upon dozens of tasks; therefore, you need a method of categorising the tasks to help determine what needs to be tackled first. To begin with, you should categorise the tasks in the following two ways:

- **De-risking activities** – to protect the wealth you currently have in your business, personal life and finances, as well as to ensure the business is operating as efficiently and effectively as possible.

- **Growth activities** – to develop your business, personal life and finances to grow your wealth.

Most of the tasks categorised as 'de-risking' will be tackled first in the Control phase. Only when you've done that are you ready to address the tasks considered 'growth activities'.

There are two reasons for starting with de-risking activities:

1. Up to this point in your life, you have built up a certain amount of wealth, both personally and within your business. You start with de-risking activities because you need to ensure this wealth is protected before moving on to the growth phase. Any growth is risky, but you can reduce this risk by making sure as many areas as possible have been de-risked before working on growth.

2. You cannot build on weak foundations. The main purpose of the de-risking phase is to strengthen any weaknesses within the three legs of your stool. There is little point in working hard to grow your business, only to watch it go bankrupt

because you didn't have a handle on the key cash flow drivers, for example. There is no value in preparing for exit without ensuring you are first prepared for the 7 Ds. In the same way, there is no sense in growing your personal wealth when you do not have a will, power of attorney or a tax-efficient vehicle in place, all of which fall under de-risking activities. I'm sure you get the idea!

Once you have prepared and secured your three plans through the de-risking process, you can then start growing and improving each plan. We separate these two categories because it is imperative that your business is de-risked before you invest time, effort and finances into growth activities. For many business owners, the intuitive way to develop and build their business is to grow it by working hard to increase sales and marketing. However, if the business is not structured in such a way to cope with or maximise on an increase in sales, or if the administrative side of the business is not in order, the time, effort and money invested in growth can be in vain. As mentioned above, a lack of cash flow control can lead to bankruptcy, even in a seemingly thriving business; if you and your business are unprepared for any of the 7 Ds, your hard work could go to waste should one of these life events occur; and before you focus on growing your business and, in turn, your personal wealth, you need to have your will, power of attorney and tax affairs in order. Only once you and your business have been de-risked and a stable platform for growth has been established is it worth investing in growth. Once this stability is established, you and your business will be ready for growth and you should see a much higher return for the time, effort and money invested in growth activities. In the next chapter, we explore de-risking activities in more detail, and in the following chapter we address growth activities.

Chapter 10 Takeaways

- Once you have ascertained your current location and end destination within the Clarity phase, you can move to the next phase – Control – where you begin to plan a route between the two.

- You will use the results of your Value Assessment to create a Master Action Plan (MAP) and journey through a Value Pathway.

- You have options as to how you undertake your journey:
  - Do-It-Yourself, using all the information from the Value Assessment
  - Peer-to-Peer Group, joining with others on a similar journey for support, as well as sharing of resources, experiences and expertise.
  - One-to-One, with a Business By Design approved advisor

- You will select a maximum of ten tasks from your MAP (five from your business plan and five from across your personal and financial plans) and work on these for 90 days, at which point, progress on each task is reviewed and a plan is put in place for the next 90-day cycle.

- You want to avoid the 'scattergun' or 'ostrich' approaches and create a focused, strategic plan to enable you to work systematically through your tasks.

- You can use Business By Design's Value Assessment tool to process your responses to the Value Assessment questions and produce for you a sequenced MAP. Contact hello@businessbydesign.co.uk for further information.

- So that you protect your wealth and establish a stable, balanced platform for growth, there is a particular order that tasks should be categorised into and then actioned:
  - De-risking activities
  - Growth activities

PHASE 2: CONTROL

CHAPTER 11

MAP and De-Risking

DE-RISKING IS VITAL, not only to add value to each leg of your three-legged stool, but also to form the solid foundation from which to grow. The primary focus of de-risking is to protect the wealth you currently have, from a business, personal and financial point of view.

De-risking is the first step in building value, and it is also the easiest to implement. We'll go through each leg of the three-legged stool individually so you can start this de-risking process as soon as possible. To repeat, this de-risking process <u>must</u> happen first because growing a business is not easy. It is risky and takes a lot of work so we must ensure that there are firm foundations in place so that the time, effort and finances invested in growth result in the best possible return. De-risking all three areas – business, personal and financial – will allow you to be as prepared as possible for most eventualities and will give you the best chance of success once you move on to growing your business.

Business De-Risking

Before any growth activities and strategies are implemented, it is critical that the business is first de-risked from an operational perspective. We do this by assessing the business's foundations. It would be extremely risky and foolish to implement a growth strategy, to turn on the sales and marketing tap, without first gaining a clear understanding of how the business is performing.

Therefore, we need to understand how the business is working from an operational point of view, as well as assess whether the foundations are strong enough to allow the business to grow. We will first look at de-risking with regard to business operations and then business foundations.

De-Risking with Regard to Business Operations

This aspect of de-risking looks at everything that could affect the operational part of the business as well as assessing any changes or developments that need to take place whilst aiming for minimal disruption. The intention here is to ensure any processes or procedures within the business operations are working as effectively and efficiently as possible.

Shareholder agreements

When de-risking business operations, I often come across outdated shareholder agreements or, in some cases, no shareholder agreements at all. If there are other directors or owners within your business, you must have a document outlining what has been agreed upon, confirmed procedures and how problems are to be resolved. One of these confirmed procedures should be a buy/sell agreement, outlining what will happen when one director, partner, or shareholder wishes to leave the business. A clear and amicable procedure must be discussed and agreed beforehand This is especially pertinent if there are significant age gaps between the respective parties. If business partners have different timelines in mind for when they may move on to their next venture or retire, where will the money come from to pay off the departing partner(s)? Who will do the work to ensure business continuity? How do the remaining partner(s) fairly compensate or buy out the exiting partner(s) without handicapping the business? How do you make a departure amicable and avoid contention? Do you have a partners' contract of commitment, requirements and constraints? Planning for transition takes consideration and planning from the outset of the business. Identify all partners' or founders' criteria and timelines early. Document the business continuity plan for each of the partners or shareholders and start preparing. If your company is a family-run business, it is still crucial to ensure that all shareholders and/or family members are on the same page.

General business considerations

For general business considerations, do all owners and senior management personnel know the location of all major documents and contracts? Is there more than one person who knows certain passwords (or where they are stored), where the lock box key is kept, or what the safe combination is?

Other de-risking areas to consider are:
- Health and safety
- Human resources
- Physical security
- Information security
- Business continuity
- Environmental and sustainability
- Finance
- Sales and marketing
- General data protection regulation (GDPR)
- Fraud
- Transport
- Quality control
- Payment card industry (PCI)
- Buildings
- Anti-money laundering
- Procurement and supply
- Directors
- Storage and warehouse
- Insurance
- Key people
- Information technology
- Business debt

For each of these areas, you will need to consider: the storage of and access to any documentation; the required knowledge of the area, how it operates and schedules for when things need reviewing/renewing; the key personnel who are involved in or responsible for the area; finances related to the area, etc. In taking time to consider and document these operations, you will be creating an operations manual for your business which, as we have discussed in previous chapters, can play a pivotal role in you becoming the CEO of your business as well as increase its transferable value.

Now that we have addressed how we would go about de-risking the operational side of a business, we now need to assess how the foundation of the business is performing in order to identify any de-risking potential there.

De-Risking in Terms of Business Foundations

Fundamental to understanding a business is to have a handle on the financials. Trying to run a business without proper and accurate financial data is like trying to drive a car whilst looking in the rear-view mirror blindfolded. The chances of successfully arriving at your destination are zero, and so it is with your business. Without accurate real-time bookkeeping, realistic and measurable forecasting and a healthy cash flow, it is inevitable that the business will either barely survive or, at some point, will wither and die. So let's look at how to de-risk and gain Control in those three areas.

Real-Time Bookkeeping

The saying, 'Garbage in, garbage out', applies to bookkeeping. Bookkeeping, although seen by many as a bit of a pain or a chore, is actually a vital part of a business. In fact, I would go as far as to say that it forms part of the fundamental foundations of a business. As the business owner, you need accurate and up-to-date financial information as and when you need it. Without accurate bookkeeping, you will get faulty or out-of-date financial information, making it virtually impossible to review, forecast or plan. Before we can start to look at any growth activities, it is imperative that the company's bookkeeping is assessed to ensure that all the nominals are coded correctly and the information being inputted is both accurate and done in real-time. With cloud accounting, there is no reason for the bookkeeping to be any more than a couple of weeks behind, ideally no more than a week behind. This will enable accurate financial reporting and allow for quick and informed decisions to be made.

Three-Way Five-Year Forecasting

What gets measured gets done, and you cannot measure what you cannot see. Using the company's profit and loss, balance sheet and cash flow statements, your accountant should be able to create a three-way five-year forecast for you. This will then be actively measured against your performance, either on a monthly or quarterly basis. This will give you the optics you need to run your business and make educated decisions.

By assessing your company's performance against budget and looking beyond the horizon, you can start to plan for your future needs. This keeps you on the front foot – a good place to be! However, this will take time and financial know-how to implement so, if you aren't confident with numbers or this level of financial detail, please speak with your accredited Business By Design advisor, who will be willing and able to assist you in creating and managing this forecast. To work with a Business By Design advisor, contact **hello@businessbydesign.co.uk** for further information or to book a discovery call.

Cash Flow

I have left the best for last! You may know the saying, 'Turnover is vanity, profit is sanity, but cash flow is reality'? In my book, *The Cash Flow Code*, I go into a lot more detail, showing you why this is so important and why you should not simply look to grow your business without first gaining a clear understanding of how strong your businesses foundations are. In the book, I give you a real-life example, using the Cash Flow Simulator, of what can happen if you do not follow this process of first ensuring your business is operating and running as efficiently as possible.

Cash flow focuses on both your balance sheet and profit and loss statements by taking the six keys that control cash flow – debtor days, creditor days, stock days, expenses, cost of sales (COS)/cost of goods sold (COGS) and sales – and ensures they are operating as effectively and efficiently as possible. In contrast to the example I lay out in *The Cash Flow Code* of what can happen if we do not first pay attention to the efficacy and efficiency of the 'six keys', by using your financial information to analyse your cash flow and improve any under-performing areas you will contribute to the firm foundations that are needed for effective long-term growth.

You can read more about gaining control of these six cash flow keys in my book, The Cash Flow Code. I have also created an online tool – the Cash Flow Simulator – which can be used to calculate and assess your current cash flow and simulate how changes to the six keys would impact future cash flow, enabling you to strategically plan based on real information. For free access to this tool, please visit **www.thesmarterexit.com**

As we have seen in this business de-risking section, by assessing and analysing your business operations and foundations and then using this information to make necessary repairs or adjustments, you will sure up the core of your business, putting it in a far stronger position to grow and receive a greater return on investment. This part of the process is all about working smarter, not harder.

We will now turn our attention to personal de-risking, an often-neglected part of a business owner's life.

Personal De-Risking

Many business owners are great at creating a vision, setting goals and planning for the future when focusing on their business. However, when it comes to their personal life, it often takes a backseat as it does not appear to be as important or critical. I would like to suggest that focusing on personal visions, goals and plans is of equal importance to the focus we devote to visions, goals and plans for our business. Time should be set aside to focus on your personal visions, goals and objectives for the future, both short and long term. As discussed in chapter 7, what are your interests outside of your business? Who are you outside of your business? Ultimately, what makes you *you*?

This personal aspect of the exit planning process is often overlooked. Having a business is, at times, all-consuming, requiring a tremendous amount of nurturing, devotion and energy, which potentially causes the owner to forsake other areas of their life that are necessary for creating balance. Over time, the owner's sole interest is their business. They find their identity and their purpose is tied to their company. When they exit the business, after the stress, excitement and relief subside, the owner is very often left aimless, without a vision of who they are or what they want to do. This can lead to a total loss of purpose and identity.

It's similar to post-wedding blues. There is often so much focus, stress, busyness and excitement in preparing for the wedding day that the couple forget that the wedding is just the event to mark the start of married life for them! The focus should be on preparing for an exciting and successful lifelong marriage that lasts long *after* the wedding is over!

This won't always be the case. Some business owners will know exactly what they want in life and are very proactive in planning an active social life, hobbies or other projects to focus on post exit. But there are a large number of business owners who have not planned for this part of their life; they won't have something else to focus on or to keep them busy post exit. They will go from the rapid-fire world of business where they had no time to breathe to a place where their time is their own and the world is their oyster. They have more time on their hands than they have ever had which, without any focus or purpose, they could find to be a real struggle.

Therefore, the personal life section of the Value Assessment, which we discussed in chapter 7, should highlight any areas for development in your personal life that you may not have thought of. The Control and Consistency phases will allow you to start putting plans in place to address any imbalances so that when you do exit your business, and even during your journey towards exit, you will find purpose in areas outside of your work.

Sticking with the de-risking process for now, in this section, we'll uncover and bring into sharp focus the aspects of your personal life that need to be de-risked so that no matter what life may throw at you, you can maintain balance and stability in your life.

Personal de-risking falls into two categories:
- Forced Exit
- Unforced Exit

Personal De-Risking: Forced Exit

A forced exit could happen during any phase of life and could be triggered by any five out of the 7 Ds that we discussed earlier: distress, disagreement, disease/disability, divorce and death. Are you prepared for these? Do you have contingencies in place? These are vital questions that require answers before we can embark on the growth phase.

Contingency planning is an area that most business owners would rather avoid and ignore. Who really wants to think about worst-case, 'what-if' scenarios? However, taking swift action to address these scenarios, involving key family members and business management teams, and documenting everything will have an immediate positive impact on the value of your business. Doing so will give any prospective buyer or investor the security and confidence that your business is a viable concern and that measures are in place to handle any unforeseen eventualities.

We have previously discussed the 7 Ds that may occur in life and affect the time and way that we exit our business. As business owners, we need to be prepared for all of these 7 Ds, even though some are not pleasant to think about. That said, in order to provide the best for your family and to build a successful business that can be passed down as your legacy, it is crucial that the five of the 7 Ds that may cause a forced exit are fully considered and addressed, thus de-risking yourself and your business, should any of these eventualities occur. The five of the 7 Ds that could force an exit are:

Distress

There are times when the business could be in distress or you may be struggling to cope with the demands and pressures of owning and running your company. A focused plan and a team around you, who are not directly linked to your business, will become a vital resource you can tap into. Without this resource, you might continue with the business and burn yourself out, or you may end up exiting the business prematurely without being able to realise the return you had hoped for. Every situation is different, but surrounding yourself with as much outside, unbiased support as possible will give you the best chance of making informed, considered and balanced decisions.

Disagreement

Founders and partners in a business are like spouses in a marriage: they do not agree on everything, nor is this necessary for the business to thrive. However, major unforeseen disagreements can cause rifts in the organisation that could harm the company, the team and even client relationships. Before an issue arises, it would be wise to create policies and procedures early on regarding how critical disagreements will be worked through. Critical disagreements may centre around issues such as: reinvesting for growth or taking dividends, how to structure the company for benefits or taxes, when to sell, which buyer option to pursue, etc. Drawing up an agreement in advance of any issues arising will align everyone's expectations and create a procedure or a structure to address and resolve these disagreements effectively.

Disease, Disability or Family Tragedies

Generally speaking, before the age of 65, we're all more likely to need the benefits of disability or critical illness insurance than to need life insurance. Here again, look at the worst-case scenario and what resources – both financially and physically – you could need. This will ensure your family will be adequately covered and provided for. As with death, there are insurance policies that can be used to offset this risk, both at a personal level as well as a business level.

From a business point of view, you'll need to ensure that all shareholders and the management team know the processes and procedures, should you be diagnosed with an illness or become injured in some way. Topics to discuss would be: who would take over the running of the business in the short term, what remunerations are to be made and for how long, etc. I would recommend adding these plans to the shareholders' agreement.

Divorce

Divorce is a costly event in itself and you would not want your business to suffer as a result, should you or a business partner get divorced. It is critical to protect the business and understand what is required from a legal perspective, so enlist the help of a specialist solicitor and make provisions to protect yourself and your business.

Death

Like taxes, death is unavoidable. Rather than deny it, think about the consequences your death will have on your business and, subsequently, on your family. There are a variety of insurance products to mitigate the financial risks of your death. You must also consider how the shareholders' agreement has been set up and what would happen in the event of your death. Using a business advisor, corporate solicitor, wealth planner and an IFA (independent financial advisor) will ensure protection of your estate and a continuity plan for your business.

No one ever wants to consider any of the 5 Ds: distress, disagreement, disease/disability, divorce, or death – as a possible risk to their business when all is going well. However, like taking out insurance, contingency planning is about making strategic decisions for eventualities that we hope will never happen, but if they do, you will be prepared. Planning for the 5 Ds is effectively an insurance policy for you and your business; we hope we will never need to activate it, but in the eventuality that we do, it makes a difficult situation somewhat easier for those involved and we are glad we considered and planned in advance. Be as detailed as you can; document each area and enlist the help of specialists to advise on specific details and the best course of action. This is how you can reduce the risk to your business and ensure its continuity if ever it is faced with any of the 5 Ds.

Personally De-Risking: Unforced Exit

An unforced exit is where you choose when to exit your business. It's when you have the luxury to choose when, where and how your exit happens. This makes up the remaining two out of the 7 Ds: deal and decide. Be aware, though, that either of these can also backfire if they have not been adequately prepared for on a business, personal or financial level.

Deal

As discussed earlier, you may be contacted out of the blue by a potential buyer. If your business is exit ready, then you'll be in a perfect position to choose whether to sell or not. It may or may not be for the amount you were hoping for, but it could mean you can grab yourself a new opportunity, should you wish to do so. Therefore, being exit ready in advance of any such offer provides you with the ability to choose whether to accept or not based on your plans rather than on the basis that your company is not ready for sale.

Decide

You may have reached a point in your life where you decide that you want to exit. All the preparation you have done up to this point will provide you with as many options as possible. You'll be ready, you will know exactly what you'll be doing post exit and you'll be financially prepared.

Since half of all business owners will be forced to exit their business and we simply do not know which half of that statistic we'll fall into, it would be wise to prepare for both types of exits. As the saying goes, 'Plan for the best and prepare for the worst', and so it must be for us – to plan for an unforced exit but, at the same time, be prepared for any forced exits.

At this point in the de-risking process, we have focused on de-risking the organisation and foundations of our business and we have prepared and put measures in place to cater for either a forced or unforced exit. It is now time to turn our attention to the final plan – our financial plan.

Financial De-Risking

Growth is not easy; it's also risky. To grow, you'll likely need to put assets at risk (which could include your personal wealth), take on debt, add people, add machinery and expand facilities. You may even need to strategically acquire another company. Understanding your tolerance for risk, along with your willingness to complete actions that protect you financially, is imperative before you begin to build value through strategic growth investments.

Understanding and protecting your wealth as much as possible is vitally important, as is understanding where you stand, your tolerances with regards to risk, your personal wealth and what you need to do to achieve financial security.

As discussed in chapter 8, you need to know Your Number: the amount of money you need to be able to retire and live the lifestyle you want, without the fear of running out of money. So many people think they know what this number is, but most of the time that number is either too high, meaning they stay in the business longer than they need to and possibly miss out on exiting at an opportune time, or that number is too low, resulting in them being unable to bridge their wealth gap in time for exit or exiting with less than they need and running out of money. Both of these outcomes are undesirable, leading to an owner spending longer in their business than they really want or intend to or being unable to live the life they had hoped for post exit, so it is important to have this dialled in and to know exactly what your target number is and what your financial requirements are.

Calculating the extent of your wealth gap will require you to know and understand your current financial position as well as Your Number. Once you know this starting point and destination, you can work with your wealth planner to create a personal investment strategy to help move you closer to your goal and gain a better understanding of how your business can bridge the wealth gap.

Your wealth planner will look at areas such as:
- Investment portfolio diversification
- Your personal loans or debt
- Any large expenses required in the future, such as paying for weddings, second homes, holidays, university fees, etc.
- Long-term care requirements
- Income requirements post transition (i.e., if standard of living adjustments are needed)
- Financial needs vs financial wants
- Net proceeds analysis: what you keep is what matters most

- Tax and estate planning
- Risk sensitivity analysis and profile
- Alignment between personal plan and business plan (wealth planner and business advisor work together to determine this)

Every person is different and will require a unique plan, but there are areas that will be common to all, especially when it comes to de-risking your personal finances. Questions to consider include the following:

- Do you have a will in place?
- Have you arranged power of attorney?
- Do you have correct and updated insurance policies in place, such a critical illness cover, life insurance, funeral policies, etc.?
- Is your estate as tax efficient as possible?
- Have you created a 'little blue file'?

The 'little blue file' is either a digital or a physical file. Whichever form you wish to use, I would recommend that the file remain offline and be kept in a safe. This file documents all your personal information, such as passwords, bank account details, investment information, policies, email accounts, utility suppliers, subscriptions, etc. In the event of your death or incapacitation, a loved one can access it and will have available to them all the information they require to sort out your estate. I have seen how difficult this can be when someone dies unexpectedly, and the people left behind struggle to access everything that they set up. The 'little blue file' is there to make this extremely difficult time as simple and smooth as possible. It is also important to remember to keep all the information updated, at least on an annual basis, to ensure all the information and documentation is accurate and up to date.

Although addressing these topics is something very few of us want to deal with, it does form part of the overall de-risking phase. Albeit uncomfortable, it is something I would encourage you to do, if not for yourself, then for your loved ones.

Understanding your personal financials and the plans you have in place will then feed into your business strategy, enabling you to look beyond the horizon and plan finances and timelines according to what you want from your exit. Coupled with this, it is good to understand how your sector will perform in the future and the possible market risks so that you can time your exit to take best advantage of any upcoming peaks in the market. Being able to see three to five years ahead will allow you to plan appropriately and will help you to time your exit accordingly in order to capture the best return on investment.

The whole de-risking process, from a business, personal and financial perspective, will take time. The most critical areas – such as writing a will, arranging power of attorney and identifying any areas within the business that could be detrimental to its continuation – need to be addressed first. Once these critical areas have been dealt with, the remaining areas can be implemented over time and combined with some growth process activities (as presented in the next chapter). Every business and every owner is different, so the timing and method of when and how you choose to start the growth phase will be up to you. Once the critical de-risking tasks are complete, you may wish to dovetail some of the remaining, less critical de-risking tasks with the beginnings of your growth activities.

This brings us to the second process in the Control phase: the growth tasks.

Chapter 11 Takeaways

De-risking activities fall into three main categories:
- Business:
  - De-risking business operations
  - De-risking business foundations
- Personal:
  - De-risking – forced exit (five of the 7 Ds)
  - De-risking – unforced exit (two of the 7 Ds)
- Financial:
  - Know your wealth gap
  - Ensuring all insurances are adequate and up to date

PHASE 2: CONTROL

CHAPTER 12

MAP and Growth

THE GROWTH PROCESS of the Control phase is undertaken in much the same way as the de-risking process. Using your Master Action Plan, you will first establish all the areas for growth in your business, and then move on to address areas for growth in your personal and financial plan. If we return to the analogy of property development, clutter must be sorted out and structural repairs dealt with first, to ensure that the property is safe and secure, before extensions are added, layouts reworked, or interiors designed in order to add value. By working through these two processes of the Control phase (de-risking and growth) in all three aspects (business, personal and financial), you will be creating a sound and strategic exit plan. And remember: Exit planning not only benefits you when you do decide the time is right to exit your business, but it helps you to gain Control of your business in the meantime, releasing you from the day-to-day running to become the CEO of your company and enabling your business to grow and flourish, providing you with a higher return both in the short term and upon your exit.

Business Growth

Before undertaking growth activities, there are several key performance indicators (KPIs) that need to be looked at first. For any growth to have the maximum benefit-to-effort ratio, these lead KPIs need to be operating as efficiently as possible:

- Margin
- Customer attrition and acquisition
- Gap analysis
- Number of transactions and transaction value

We'll cover each of these lead KPIs as we look at business growth.

Margin

Improving margins by very small amounts across the business will have a huge impact on its overall profitability. The first knee-jerk reaction to improving margins is to increase prices, which we can do and will most certainly look at doing during the growth phase, but there are many other ways to improve margins. I do appreciate that, for some businesses, pricing is very sensitive and that a strategy to simply increase prices won't work for them. Therefore, we'll look at other areas within the business that can contribute to increased margins.

The quickest way to improve your gross margin is to stop offering discounts. Discounts are the quickest way to destroy margins. Let me give you an example:

Current Margin Rate

		20%	25%	30%	35%	40%	45%	50%	55%	60%
	2%	11%	9%	7%	6%	5%	5%	4%	4%	3%
	4%	25%	19%	15%	13%	11%	10%	9%	8%	7%
	6%	43%	32%	25%	21%	18%	15%	14%	12%	11%
	8%	67%	47%	36%	30%	25%	22%	19%	17%	15%
	10%	100%	67%	50%	40%	33%	29%	25%	22%	20%
	12%	150%	92%	67%	52%	43%	36%	32%	28%	25%
	14%	233%	127%	88%	67%	54%	45%	39%	34%	30%
	16%	400%	178%	114%	84%	67%	55%	47%	41%	36%
	18%	900%	257%	150%	106%	82%	67%	56%	49%	43%
	20%	x	400%	200%	133%	100%	80%	67%	57%	50%
	25%	x	x	500%	250%	167%	125%	100%	83%	71%
	30%	x	x	x	600%	300%	200%	150%	120%	100%

Amount of Discount Applied

To produce the same profit, you must INCREASE your sales volume by:

If we assume your gross margin rate is 30% and you were to offer a standard 10% discount to drum up extra sales, that would mean that in order to achieve the same level of profit, you would have to increase your sales volume by 50%! The question to ask yourself is, will offering that 10% discount increase the sales volume by more than 50%? If not, it is certainly not worth the time and energy offering it, not to mention the potential problems it could cause for your cash flow.

Rather, look at your current products or services and create a premium offering that has a high perceived value for the customer – one which they cannot find anything similar to in the marketplace.

Upsell at All Times

Ensure all staff, or at least the sales team, know how to upsell to a customer. 'Would you like fries with that?' makes McDonald's millions every year. Upselling exists in many forms, but the principle remains the same: offer customers the opportunity to purchase additional items to benefit, enhance, supplement, or otherwise improve upon their current purchase or experience. Strategic entrepreneurs understand that customers are far more likely to increase their purchase while already in 'buying mode'. Look at your business and see how you could do any of the following:

- Create an incentive to purchase more products. This could be in the form of a financial incentive, additional products or the promise of improving the chance of a successful outcome or result.

- Look to add accessories to your main products or services.

- Provide a product or service that protects the customer's purchase. This could be in the form of insurance or maintenance plans.

- Offer or show the customer what other people have bought when purchasing particular items. (*Customers who bought this also bought…* or *If you like this, you might also like…*) This could not only help spark an idea in the customer's mind, but it is also a chance to show what other products or services you offer.

Bundle products or services together to create a high value offering that no competitor can provide. Customers will be less focused on price and more focused on the value they are receiving.

Negotiate with suppliers both on terms and price or look for new suppliers. This is something that needs to be done at least once a year.

Increase Prices

I know at the start of this section I acknowledged that increases in pricing may not be possible for all businesses; however, being strategic about it will not only increase your margin but also make your life a lot easier. You could either increase prices across the board if that would work for your business or you could look to only increase prices for those customers that we refer to as D-grade customers. These are the customers who take up most of your time and resources, don't pay on time, negotiate over price, complain, etc. Increasing prices only for D-grade customers will either cause them to leave, or if they choose to stay, they will be making it worth your while.

Should you be hesitant to increase prices for fear of losing customers, let me show you an example of what could happen:

Current Margin Rate

Amount of Price Increase Applied	20%	25%	30%	35%	40%	45%	50%	55%	60%
2%	9%	7%	6%	5%	5%	4%	4%	4%	3%
4%	17%	14%	12%	10%	9%	8%	7%	7%	6%
6%	23%	19%	17%	15%	13%	12%	11%	10%	9%
8%	29%	24%	21%	19%	17%	15%	14%	13%	12%
10%	33%	29%	25%	22%	20%	18%	17%	15%	14%
12%	38%	32%	29%	26%	23%	21%	19%	18%	17%
14%	41%	36%	32%	29%	26%	24%	22%	20%	19%
16%	44%	39%	35%	31%	29%	26%	24%	23%	21%
18%	47%	42%	38%	34%	31%	29%	26%	25%	23%
20%	50%	44%	40%	36%	33%	31%	29%	27%	25%
25%	56%	50%	45%	42%	38%	36%	33%	31%	29%
30%	60%	55%	50%	46%	43%	40%	38%	35%	33%

To produce the same profit, you could DECREASE your sales volume by:

By taking the same example previously, this table above shows what could happen if instead of offering a 10% discount you *increase* prices by 10%. Should this happen, you could afford to lose 25% of your customers and still produce the same amount of profit. That potentially means 25% less hassle – 25% less work for the same amount of profit. The question to ask yourself is: If you did increase your prices by 10%, will there be a chance of losing one in every four of your customers? I would think the chances are small, but it does give you an idea of what you could do and, once again, provides you with options.

Customer Attrition and Acquisition

This is a vital KPI to know, understand and monitor. Every business owner must have a system in place to know how many customers they are losing and gaining each year. This knowledge will highlight whether the advertising and marketing spend is producing a return and which advertising and marketing activities are actually working. By knowing what is and what is not working, you can invest your money in the things that are making a return on investment. This will have a huge impact on the profitability of your business.

Gap Analysis

As business owners, we all know the depth and breadth of products and services we offer – we live and breathe them every day – but do our customers know? Carrying out a gap analysis will highlight any areas within your offering where your customers aren't buying from you. This would be a good opportunity to arrange a meeting with customers to explain everything you offer. Many customers may not be aware of everything you do, and this will be an opportunity to showcase everything you have to offer them, with the additional benefit of creating another touch point with customers where you can also learn if there is anything irritating or not going well for them that can be resolved. Who knows? You could even get a testimonial.

Number of Transactions and Transaction Value

In addition to customer attrition and acquisition, knowing the number of transactions and the average transaction value is extremely important. We first need to establish whether these numbers are

188 THE SMARTER EXIT • Cliff Spolander

increasing or decreasing. Once that is established, we are then able to find ways of improving these numbers using the gap analysis above and monitoring how many customers we're gaining and losing each year. With this knowledge in hand, we can then look at the business's overall product or service offering to determine how we can increase both the number of transactions and the transaction value for each customer.

As the owner of the business, you will also need to decide whether you wish to build an owner-centric business that creates a nice lifestyle for you, or a value-centric business that creates transferable value and provides you with the most options when exiting. Chapter 14 addresses this essential issue specifically, providing strategies for you to shift your business from being owner- to value-centric.

Personal and Financial Growth Activities

As previously presented in chapter 7, the 14 areas that affect our personal lives include the following:

- Achievement
- Business
- Character
- Emotional state
- Exit preparation
- Fun and recreation
- Health and fitness
- Intellectual development
- Life vision
- Love relationship
- Personal blocks
- Post-exit plans
- Quality of life
- Social life

It is during the growth process of the Control phase that you'll start to address each of these areas and begin to emotionally detach yourself from your business and, looking beyond it, create a life for yourself outside of your work. Some owners will have several of these areas already dialled in, yet many won't. To be in the best possible position for exiting your business, it is vital that you start to look at your life in these areas and begin shaping what your life will become post exit.

At this point, your wealth planner and tax advisor will play a very important role, working with you to ensure your affairs are as tax efficient as possible and that your personal wealth, along with your business finance, is working hard for you to contribute to bridging any wealth gap that you may have. Remember: You must not solely rely on your business to bridge this wealth gap; as none of us knows what the future may bring, finance balanced with preparedness is the key to your success.

Every person is different, so each individual will require a unique plan. Therefore, it is difficult for me to go into any depth as to precisely what you personally need to do without you first taking the personal and financial readiness questionnaire. However, as already discussed, it will be hugely beneficial for you to look at and create an achievable plan for all these areas of your life and to appoint a wealth and tax planner to assist you.

The goal here is to bridge any wealth gap as quickly as possible with the aim of you reaching your exit number sooner than you envisage. This will buy you time – time that you choose how to spend. This is the magic of exit planning and why having a team around you is so important.

In the next chapter, we'll be looking at all the activities that we have already listed under the headings of de-risking tasks and growth tasks, and this time, we will subdivide them within a value versus cost matrix. As you'll learn, doing so allows you to create the ideal sequence for the de-risking and growth activities you'll be pursuing.

Chapter 12 Takeaways

- So that the maximum benefit-to-effort ratio can be gained from business growth activities, the following lead key performance indicators (KPIs) need to be looked at first to ensure they are operating efficiently and to make any necessary changes:
  - Margin
  - Customer attrition and acquisition
  - Gap analysis
  - Number of transactions and transaction value

- You need to decide whether you wish to build an owner-centric (lifestyle) business or a value-centric business and take the appropriate action accordingly. (More about this in chapter 14.)

- For personal and financial growth, we must improve the 14 areas that affect our personal lives, including the following:
  - Achievement
  - Business
  - Character
  - Emotional state
  - Exit preparation
  - Fun and recreation
  - Health and fitness
  - Intellectual development
  - Life vision
  - Love relationship
  - Personal blocks
  - Post-exit plans
  - Quality of life
  - Social life

- Through these growth activities and in conjunction with your wealth planner, the aim is to bridge the wealth gap as soon as possible so that you are ready for exit as early as possible – be that forced or unforced.

MAP and Value vs Cost Matrix

IN THE PREVIOUS CHAPTERS, we have explored the activities that form the Master Action Plan (MAP) and considered these activities under the two headings of de-risking tasks and growth tasks. We learned the importance of starting with the critical de-risking tasks to shore up the foundations of the business and ensure it has a stable and efficient structure to withstand growth. Once we have a secure foundation on which to build, we can begin to action the growth tasks that will help to grow the business, increase sales and take the company to the next level. To enable us to plan a cycle of de-risking and growth activities, we need to weigh up the cost of each task against the value that it will bring. In this chapter, we will explore how to ascertain value versus cost and how to find the ideal balance of the two for your business.

Once you have categorised all tasks on your MAP into the two main categories – de-risking and growth – each activity then needs to be placed into a value versus cost matrix so that you can weigh up the cost of each task against the potential value that it will add to your business. As you'll soon learn, categorising the tasks with this matrix helps to sequence the tasks optimally.

Value vs Cost Matrix

The value vs cost matrix comprises two axes – value and cost – which intersect to form a four-part matrix. Each task within the de-risking and growth processes is analysed as to the value it will bring to your business, personal and financial plans against the cost of implementation and can then be plotted along the value/cost axes and placed into the relevant quadrant of the matrix. This provides an overview of all the MAP tasks and where they sit in the value vs cost comparison, enabling you to plan your sequence of tasks within each 90-day cycle.

The matrix looks like this:

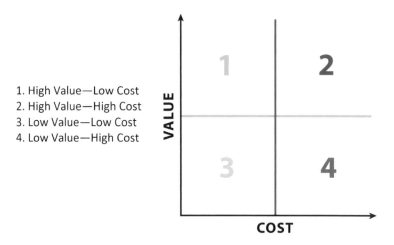

1. High Value—Low Cost
2. High Value—High Cost
3. Low Value—Low Cost
4. Low Value—High Cost

When it is time to sequence the activities from your MAP into a shorter-term plan for each 90-day cycle, as you'll see, it makes the most sense to first focus on the **high value—low cost** and the **high value—high cost** activities (quadrants 1 and 3 of the matrix). Why? Because these are the 'low-hanging fruit', meaning that accomplishing these tasks will have a big impact on your three plans whilst initially requiring a lower investment of cash and other resources. Once these tasks are completed, you then move on to the **low value—low-cost** activities (in quadrant 3 of the matrix). Once these are all completed, you can choose to either disregard or focus your attention on the tasks that are **low value—high cost** (quadrant 4 of the matrix). These are the 'nice-to-haves' but bring little value to your overall plans so, after completing the tasks in the other three quadrants, you may choose to discard these tasks or to complete some or all of them, if you have the time and resources to do so.

To exemplify, let's explore the types of activities that fall into the four quadrants of the matrix.

Quadrant 1: Examples of High Value—Low Cost

De-Risking Activities:

- **Business Plan:**
  - Improve cash flow.
  - Undertake an employee engagement workshop – from there you'll find even more high value tasks that you could undertake.
  - Obtain enhanced the financial management reporting from your accountant or finance team.

- **Personal Plan:**
  - Create a personal plan for life post exit.

- **Financial Plan:**
  - Engage with a reputable wealth and tax planner.

Growth Activities:

- **Business Plan:**
  - Carry out a customer analysis to understand who your customers are and what they are buying from you
  - Implement business and cash flow modelling.
  - Carry out a performance and supplier analysis

- **Personal Plan:**
  - Start to implement your personal plans.

- **Financial Plan:**
  - Create a personal investment strategy.

Quadrant 2: Examples of High Value–High Cost

De-Risking Activities:

- **Business Plan:**
  - Create a standard operations manual.
  - Review all legal, IP, and trademark documentation.
  - Bring on board consultants in human resources, information technology, virtual finance directorship, CRM systems, etc.

- **Personal Plan:**
  - Get a full health check. This may need to be carried out privately.
  - Write down all the relationships in your life in which you need to invest.

- **Financial Plan:**
  - Use the business to help bridge the wealth gap.

Growth Activities:

- **Business Plan:**
  - Use capital resources to improve operational efficiency.
  - Change the culture of the business.
  - Establish employee acquisition and retention strategies.

- **Personal Plan:**
  - Enlist the help of a personal trainer and dietitian to support you in looking after your body.
  - Start investing in your relationships. This may not necessarily be high cost in monetary terms, but it could require an investment of time.

Quadrant 3: Examples of Low Value—Low Cost

De-Risking Activities:

- **Business Plan:**
  - Reducing insurance premiums.
  - Utilities management.
  - Company formation paperwork.

Growth Activities:

- **Business Plan:**
  - Improving market position or strength.
  - Strategic alignment.
  - Office & warehouse space.

Quadrant 4: Examples of Low Value—High Cost

General Activities:

- **Business Plan:**
  - Buy newer office furniture.
  - Offer bigger and more elaborate staff parties and events.
  - Engage in different marketing activities outside of your marketing strategy.
  - Carry out a complete rebrand.
  - Move to newer premises.

You may have noticed that, in the examples given above, no tasks pertaining to your personal or financial plans fall into quadrants 3 or 4 of the value versus cost matrix – the low value—low cost and low value—high cost categories. This is because everything you do within these two plans for your personal and financial future will always be of high value. You'll need to live with yourself long after exiting your business, and any investment you make personally and financially will always be of high value.

Regardless of whether you're in the de-risking process or the growth process, you'll enter the 90-day cycle, which is continuously repeated, until you decide to exit the business. Your three plans will continually change and evolve with the ebb and flow of your business and your life and the constant cycle of de-risking and growing those three plans will create a regular rhythm and culture of continuous improvement. Every year, you will undertake an annual Value Assessment to measure the progress of your three plans over the previous 12 months, allowing you the opportunity to recognise progress and to plan accordingly for the next 12 months. You will adjust ongoing tasks and select new required tasks to work on for the coming year. This constant cycle of improving, reviewing and analysing the three areas (business, personal and financial) will keep you moving in the right direction towards your destination point. You will be securing and growing each leg of your three-legged stool so that you are preparing your business and yourself for your eventual exit, as well as becoming as prepared as you can for any unforeseen future events. Not only that but, as mentioned previously, you will start to reap the rewards of your labour during your journey. By you becoming the CEO and growing your business from these secure foundations, your business will start to run more efficiently, and you will be generating increased cash flow and building transferable value ready for exit.

Chapter 13 Takeaways

- Once you have categorised all tasks on your MAP into the two main categories – de-risking and growth – each activity then needs to be placed into a value vs cost matrix so that you can weigh up the cost of each task against the potential value that it will add to your business.

- The value vs cost matrix comprises four quadrants:
  - High Value—Low Cost
  - High Value—High Cost
  - Low Value—Low Cost
  - Low Value—High Cost

- When selecting tasks from your MAP for your 90-day cycles, start with the High Value—Low Cost and High Value—High Cost activities (the 'low-hanging fruit'), then move on to the Low Value—Low Cost and only engage in Low Value—High Cost activities if you have the time and resources to do so.

- There are no Low Value activities for personal and financial plans: any investment of time, money or resources you make for your personal or financial future will always be of high value.

- You will continue to work through your MAP on 90-day cycles until your eventual exit.

- You should begin to benefit from your work during your journey as your business begins to run more efficiently and successfully and as your time is released for you to pursue interests outside of work.

Implementing Your MAP

WE NOW ARRIVE at the part of the Control phase where it is time to begin implementing the Master Action Plan by putting into action the tasks that have been identified through the Value Assessment process and listed in your business, personal and financial plans. It may seem as if it has taken a significant amount of time to arrive at this point, the stage at which we really begin to work on all three aspects and start to effect change, but as with many things in life, higher success lies in careful preparation, and the more detailed and thorough we can be in the Value Assessment and creation of the three plans, the more specific and targeted we can be with our actions and developments, leading to more effective and impactful change. In this chapter, we will look at the steps to take when implementing the MAP for the best return on the time, effort and resources that you invest in its activities.

As we discovered in chapters 11 and 12, the first part of the Control Phase is to take your Master Action Plan (MAP) and begin to sequence it by dividing all the activities into two key categories:

- De-risking activities
- Growth activities

Once we have the activities divided into these two categories, we are then able to further divide each category, using the value vs cost matrix:

- De-Risking activities:
  - High Value—Low Cost
  - High Value—High Cost

- Low Value—Low Cost
- Low Value—High Cost

• Growth activities:
  - High Value—Low Cost
  - High Value—High Cost
  - Low Value—Low Cost
  - Low Value—High Cost

When all of the activities have been established and categorised, we can then plan how and when to implement them in a structured and ordered manner.

As every business and owner is different, which activities you choose to implement and when you decide to implement them will depend on the direction in which you are heading. You need to establish what type of business you're building – an owner-centric or value-centric business – which will determine how you go about growing it. An owner-centric business will provide the lifestyle you want, but the business itself will be centred around you, which is absolutely fine if that is your intention. What you need to bear in mind – and what I pointed out many times in part one of this book – is that this type of company depends on you being there for its continued success, which reduces its transferable value. Growing an owner-centric business would therefore be centred around the business funding your financial plan as tax efficiently as possible. This type of business is the easiest to grow, but its owner-dependence could affect the saleability of the company.

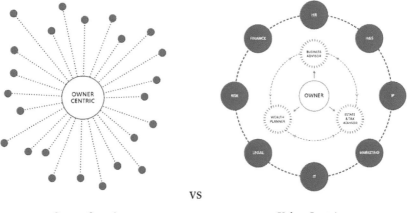

VS

Owner Centric   Value Centric

If, however, you want to build a value-centric business, it will require a different approach. It will take more time and be more challenging, but the results are worth it. When you want to exit, your value-centric business will allow you to attract the right buyer or investor for the right valuation, and should any unforeseen events occur, you'll be prepared for them because the business can function without you or can be sold relatively quickly. Part one outlined in great detail the many advantages of creating a value-centric business.

In this Control phase, as you work through the de-risking and growth processes, the culture of your business will begin to change. I would never recommend trying to change your business's culture from the start; it is simply too complex, takes a long time and is challenging to shift without changes in other aspects of the business. It is far better to allow the culture to change organically over time as you de-risk and grow your business by putting into place measures to change from an owner-centric to a value-centric business. During this time, you'll naturally shed the employees that do not buy into the new changes, thus creating the new culture, but at the same time, you will retain and attract the right people who align with what you're doing and your direction of travel. By systematically developing a practice of continuous improvement to shift your business towards being value centric, you'll automatically influence and change the culture.

Like with all changes, there is a process to follow when shifting from an owner-centric business to a value-centric business. However, this process is not written in stone and can be adapted, depending on where you and your business currently are. In the rest of this chapter, I'll outline key steps to implement in order for you to make this shift. Please note that you do not necessarily need to implement these steps in the sequence I present them. Feel free to switch them around, depending on how it most makes sense for you and your business to transition from being owner centric to value centric. The essential component is that you consistently put in the effort to make this shift so that down the line, whether your exit is forced or unforced, you will optimise that exit and be prepared for your post-exit life.

Shifting from Owner Centric to Value Centric: Some Quick Wins

The following actions will help you shift your business from being owner centric to value centric. As already stated, the sequence in which you implement these actions can vary, depending on what works best for you and your business.

Organisational Chart

An organisational chart is a diagram that visually conveys a company's internal structure by detailing the roles, responsibilities and relationships among individuals within the business. In an owner-centric business, the majority of the roles and responsibilities will be allocated to the owner themselves, whilst in a value-centric business, the chart will convey that the owner holds responsibility for any tasks relating to finances, growth and finding and nurturing talent (the roles of the company CEO), with the day-to-day management and running of the business being allocated to a management team and employees.

Begin by creating an organisational chart of how the tasks of your business are currently allocated, then create an organisational chart for how you want the organisation of your business to look in three to five years' time. In the first version of the chart, you may find that you are doing most of the work in your business as it currently functions. Thus, your business in its current form is owner centric. This is absolutely fine because the second version of the chart provides you with a plan for how to envision the allocation of these duties in the future. You can see which tasks that you currently do should be assigned to others, and you have the description of those tasks which over time you'll group together to develop complete job descriptions for those personnel who will undertake these roles.

After this, you will be ready to start building the team around your business. Look to find roles within the company that can be outsourced – roles that do not require you to take on more employees. Doing so allows you the flexibility to outsource roles to experts in their field when you need them, meaning that each role in the business is carried out by a specialist without the commitment and overhead of employing more staff than is necessary. In this way, you will create a nimbler business – one that can adapt and mould to the changes within the marketplace and even unexpected events, such as a pandemic, for that matter.

Some of the key roles you can outsource include: a bookkeeper; a part-time financial director; a human resources consultant; and an external IT company to ensure all your IT systems are supported, current and secure. You could even look to hire a virtual assistant and/or a health and safety consultant. Notice I recommend you outsource any roles that require specialised knowledge and involve keeping up with ever-changing regulations and legal requirements. Not only will this free up your time and make these important roles in your business independent of you, but because these roles will be carried out by external specialists with the responsibility of keeping abreast of developments in their field, it will also de-risk your business.

Financials

Whilst building your team, work with your bookkeeper and accountant to tidy up the financials of your business. The accountancy sector is changing, and only those accountants who are proactive and forward-thinking will survive into the new digital age. If your accountant is not proactive and they are not speaking with you at least on a quarterly basis, I would encourage you to start looking for a new accountant. One of the keys to running a successful business is understanding cash flow and the drivers that influence that KPI. You can find out more about cash flow in my book, *The Cash Flow Code*. The other key to creating accurate and timely reports hinges on your bookkeeping, ensuring everything is coded accurately and the nominals are correct. Having this real-time, up-to-date enhanced financial management reporting is critical to you being able to make informed decisions, so this is a crucial step to take.

I do appreciate that we business owners from time to time put some personal expenses through our company. I would encourage you to either stop doing that or at least minimise it as much as possible. If or when you do it, keep a detailed record of those transactions with the corresponding receipts or invoices. I recommend this because when a buyer values your business, you will want to add all those personal expenses back into the business. These expenses, called add-backs, will increase the net profit and therefore the value of the business if the seller can prove to a buyer that these expenses are not business related. Too many add-backs, however, will make a buyer suspicious, causing some add-backs to not be considered.

Operations

As your business grows and new positions start to be created, build a standard operations manual (SOP) for your company. This will act as an induction and training manual for new recruits, as well as for current employees moving roles or departments. Because everything that happens within the business will be documented, it will also make the business less reliant upon you. This manual will take time to create and will need to be updated frequently, but doing so will help you move towards a value-centric business and ultimately a higher transferable value.

A Common Vision and Purpose

Running a successful business requires having the right people in the right roles. People need something to aim for, be it a goal or higher purpose – something to focus on so that they know that what they are doing is contributing not only to their own success but to the success of the business and to a cause higher than themselves. Therefore, planning for and achieving buy-in from your team is vital. Initially, this will start at the top, or at least the top management team. As things progress, the entire company will become involved, keeping your team inspired and motivated.

As part of your company's higher purpose, and that of each member of your team, you could choose to sponsor and support a cause that aligns with the values of your business and its staff. A great starting point is to look at B1G1: Business for Good at **https://b1g1.com**, a platform that facilitates targeted giving to verified charities linked to goals and achievements accomplished by your business and your team – motivational for the business and its employees and beneficial for the chosen causes.

You can give to causes such as:
- Providing clean water to communities in Africa
- Educating local fishing and farming communities in the Philippines about sustainable practices
- Distributing equipment and appliances that run on renewable energy to rural villages in India
- Enabling students and adults around the world to continue their training and education
- Funding reforestation projects in different continents

Breaking down your five-year vision into yearly targets is a great way for your team to know what the purpose is each year so as to ensure everyone is focused on the target. However, a lot can happen over a 12-month period, and being able to adapt to any changes within the marketplace is a real advantage.

As your business grows and changes, you'll gain a thorough picture of the roles, responsibilities and activities – the pieces of the puzzle – that make up your business. This is a continual, ongoing process that won't end until you finally exit, but weaving this continual growth and development process into the very fabric of your business will create a strong culture, whatever that may look like for your company.

Using 90-Day Cycles

Ninety days is neither too long nor too short for putting into action the various tasks on your MAP towards making your business exit ready and moving it from being owner centric to value centric. This is an optimum timeframe to keep track of what is happening within your business and respond accordingly.

Because each 90-day cycle is made up of short-term highly focused objectives from your MAP, it prevents procrastination, and everyone is more likely to see results from the changes you're enacting. As such, it is also more likely to motivate those team members who may not be as engaged to follow through on their part of the Control phase. The last thing they will want is to be the only person reporting to the group that they aren't on track to accomplish their tasks. As a result, they will either toe the line and remain part of the business or they won't fit the developing culture of the company and leave. Either outcome is a good result for you; you only want staff who will identify with your company's new culture and procedures. Those that do not have no place in your business.

When you have everyone pulling in the same direction, you create momentum and increase morale. However, throughout this Control phase MAP process, things will crop up in people's personal lives and within the business. At times, it won't always be possible to complete every task. This too is okay. Focus on your 'moving average' – your overall direction of travel and progress without the complexity of detailed fluctuations. As long as some tasks are completed, you are still moving in the right direction. All that is needed is to take those incomplete tasks and carry them forward to the next 90-day cycle – the goal is just to move forward. Following this process, however – checking in with team members every month and offering accountability, encouragement and support where necessary – will greatly reduce the number of incomplete tasks in each cycle.

I always recommend that you select no more than five tasks from your business plan and no more than five tasks from across your personal and financial plans per 90-day cycle. Anything more than 10 tasks per 90 days and you run the risk of not getting them all completed in time. There may be times when you are only able to select and complete one task for that 90-day cycle – this is absolutely fine. Don't beat yourself up. Remember your moving average and ensure that on average, you are always improving over the quarter or the year. It is better to select and complete one task successfully than to select 10 and get none completed due to overwhelm. That would serve no purpose other than to demotivate, which would be counterproductive.

Having a series of 90-day cycles allows you to respond appropriately as required. This ensures there is plenty of opportunity to adapt to trends, navigate your business where necessary and work with the most current information.

Think about these 90-day cycles as HIIT (high intensity interval training) workouts for your business. Choose up to ten MAP tasks from across your business, personal and financial plans. Break those individual tasks into monthly milestones, then break those monthly milestones into weekly or daily objectives. As you consistently work through these small objectives, your progress will accumulate, enabling you to achieve your 90-day target.

Clearly communicating the aims and objectives for the next 90 days will help to prevent your team from feeling too overwhelmed. Creating focus, intention and determination for just a short period of time will allow you and your team to see results quickly, which will then encourage and motivate everyone for the next 90-day cycle.

Be 'SMARTER'

Using the Master Action Plan (MAP), breaking down tasks into de-risking and growth tasks and using the value vs cost matrix will reveal the areas to focus on first – the low-hanging fruit. To complete these tasks, I recommend using the SMARTER methodology of tackling goals. Whatever your intentions are for the next 90 days, make sure that your mission is:

S: Specific

M: Measurable

A: Attainable

R: Realistic

T: Time-based

E: Efficient

R: Resourced

Notice how this takes the well-known SMART goal method and adds on the final -ER to make it SMARTER. This is so that you as the business owner are more *efficient* and better *resourced*. This means getting yourself and/or your team to implement certain tasks. Whichever tasks are chosen, each task must have sufficient resources in order for it to be completed. Resources could be money, time, equipment, staff, etc.

Create Cohesion

Once you have chosen your 90-day cycle tasks, get your team involved. Ask for their feedback on your proposed plan. This is a great way to come up with creative solutions for any problems you might face during the cycle, and it builds accountability within your organisation as everyone will establish a firm understanding of where the company is going and what they each need to do during the next 90 days to contribute to the journey. It will also create a sense of involvement; your team members will feel seen and heard in the plans for the upcoming changes, which should result in greater enthusiasm and buy-in on their part.

Create Accountability: Take Action

Finally, once the objectives have been agreed upon, they need to be transformed into actionable steps – steps that are broken down into monthly milestones and weekly and daily objectives. Assign each task to someone within your team. Initially this may only be you, which is absolutely fine to start with. As you grow, you'll begin to create a team around you, but do not let the lack of a team stop you from taking action now!

Make each person accountable for their role in the next 90 days. Ensure that everyone knows precisely what they need to do and that they have the resources they need to accomplish their goals. Arrange weekly or monthly updates with your team where each member reports their progress to the group. This provides accountability to ensure they are on track to complete their tasks, but more importantly, it will highlight any potential problems that may have arisen during the month, so these can be addressed swiftly to avoid any delays in the work towards meeting objectives and targets.

In this chapter, we have completed our coverage of all you need to know for phase 2 of the Stabilise-Systemise-Scale Process: the Control Phase. We took the results from phase 1, the Clarity Phase (chapters 5 to 9), where we carried out the Value Assessment that helped us produce a Master Action Plan (MAP). In chapters 11 to 12, we divided the MAP into two key categories, namely de-risking and growth activities.

Once that was completed, in chapter 13, we took each task from both sections and further divided them into four categories using the value vs cost matrix: high value—low cost, high value—high cost, low value—low cost and low value—high cost.

Now that you have all your tasks divided into the relevant categories, you can prioritise the tasks that will give you the most traction to drive forward all three of your plans. Implementing this part of the process will require you as the owner to select tasks that will deliver the highest value for the lowest cost in time, money and resources. You must ensure that each task has the proper resources required to be completed within the 90-day cycle, after which the task will be reviewed and, if completed, ticked off the list. You then go back to the Master Action Plan and choose more tasks to complete for the coming 90 days. From this chapter, you also gathered more information on how to enact tasks that will shift your business from being owner centric to value centric so that you'll ultimately have the most ideal range of options when you exit, whether it is forced or unforced.

The key here is Consistency, which is phase 3 of the Stabilise-Systemise-Scale Process. It is only by Consistently working on your Master Action Plan in a very strategic and structured way that you will be able to move your business and yourself to that exit-ready position. Through Consistency you create value, which is the subject of the next chapter.

Chapter 14 Takeaways

- Before embarking on your 90-day cycles to select and action your MAP activities, you need to decide whether you are building an owner-centric or value-centric business.

- As you make changes and improvements to your business, you will notice the culture evolving organically in alignment with those changes and your personnel naturally assessing whether they themselves align with the new culture.

- Some quick wins upon shifting your business from owner centric to value centric are:
  - Creating an organisational chart.
  - Tidying up your business financials.
  - Building a standard operations manual (SOP) for your company.
  - Creating a common vision and purpose to bring the whole team on board.

- You will work through your MAP tasks in 90-day cycles, reviewing progress at the end of each cycle to tick off completed tasks and carry forward any incomplete activities.

- Don't become despondent if some tasks do not get completed within a 90-day cycle. Remember to keep track of your moving average to see your overall progress.

- Use the SMARTER approach for working on goals to ensure that tasks are completed successfully.

- Create a sense of accountability and involvement by involving your team in planning how the 90-day cycle tasks will be executed.

- Break down full tasks into monthly milestones and weekly/daily objectives. Build in regular reviews of progress towards these objectives to ensure that everyone is on track to complete as many tasks as possible in the cycle.

Value Creation

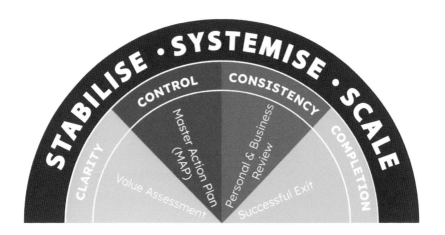

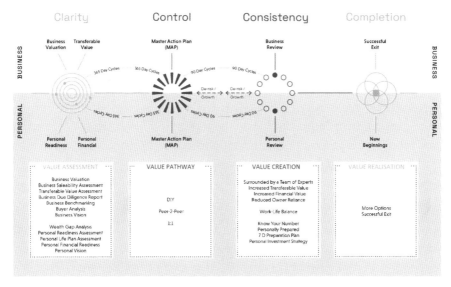

ONCE YOU HAVE gained Clarity, using your Master Action Plan (MAP), you'll be moving between Control and Consistency every 90 days. This will form the core of the Stabilise-Systemise-Scale Process. Let's delve into what exactly Consistency looks like so that you can ensure you are achieving the level of Consistency necessary to move your business to being value centric so that when it is time to exit, you have the most options available for your business, yourself and your finances.

Business & Personal Review

After each 90-day cycle, it is important to take some time to assess your progress, determine your new current position, understand what has changed in your business and in your personal life and assess any needs to factor into the next 90-day cycle. At this review, you'll find out which tasks could not be completed and the person or team responsible for any such task must provide an account as to why it was not achieved. Any tasks not completed must then be carried over to the next 90-day cycle to be actioned along with any newly added tasks taken from the MAP. Before embarking on the next 90-day cycle, all chosen tasks must be properly resourced to give those responsible the very best chance of completing them before the next review period.

As with every 90-day cycle, this next set of tasks will be broken down into shorter-term objectives with monthly check-ins to monitor progress and address any issues that may have arisen since the review.

Once four 90-day cycles have been completed, it is time to carry out another Value Assessment. This is an annual assessment to track and measure progress over the longer term. This assessment looks at how much the value of your business has increased, both from a financial and transferable value perspective. The annual Value Assessment also determines how you have progressed in both your personal life and your financial life.

Keeping track of your progression will help to establish where you are and whether you are on course. For any corrections you need to make, carrying out the assessment annually helps you to determine those changes and make those corrections sooner rather than later. This is a very proactive style of managing your business and living your life because in doing this, you're no longer at the mercy of what life may throw at you. Instead, you're in Control – changing and adapting, taking positive steps to being prepared and being on the front foot.

This process is not for everyone. It is only for those people who are serious about their business and their life – those who not only want to be the very best version of themselves, but who also want to provide a living for those they employ and secure a future for their loved ones. This process takes time, dedication and discipline, which is why having an accredited Business By Design advisor to walk alongside you is vitally important. There will be times when things aren't going well and life is hard, and it will be at those times that your advisor will encourage you and offer guidance and support.

If you would like to benefit from the 1:1 support of a Business By Design advisor or from joining a Peer-to-Peer group, please contact **hello@businessbydesign.co.uk** to find out more.

As you gain more Control and maintain your Clarity regarding where you are at and where you're heading, you'll start to create value within your three plans. For example:

Business Plan:
- You will start to create your very own team of experts around you.
- The business will become less reliant upon you, shifting from being owner centric to value centric. For those looking to sell, this means that the business will increase in both financial and transferable value.
- Irrespective of your exit strategy, you will start to create a better work-life balance.

Personal Plan:
- You will feel personally prepared for your life post exit.
- You will be prepared for any of the 7 Ds – for those curveballs that life may throw at you.

Financial Plan:

- At this point, you will know Your Number and you will have a personal investment strategy as well as a business strategy to help bridge any wealth gaps.

- You may even begin your retirement or exit plans sooner than you thought!

Having an exit strategy is like having travel insurance. None of us go on holiday with the intention of breaking a leg or getting sick. However, should any unforeseen event happen, you know that all the medical bills will be covered, and you can get back home. An exit strategy works in much the same way; it prepares your business – and it prepares you personally and financially – so that you have the very best chance of exiting your business successfully. If any unforeseen events happen, such as any of the 5 Ds, you will be prepared and have a plan in place to deal with that situation.

Having an exit strategy allows you to prepare your business, prepare yourself and protect your finances because none of us knows what is around the corner.

As you can see, this is an ongoing process; it is a marathon, not a sprint. It takes careful preparation and Consistent and extended effort. By Consistently taking action, by taking one step at a time, by being intentional and focused, you'll get there. This is what this methodology is all about. It is a proven methodology that brings Clarity, Control and focus to your business, personal and financial life.

Now that we have looked at the Clarity, Control and Consistency phases by first gaining an understanding of exactly where we are, then de-risking the businesses and then implementing strategic growth strategies over 90-day cycles, we then need to work on realising that value and using it to Complete your journey. This brings us to phase 4, the final phase of the process and the final chapter of this book.

Chapter 15 Takeaways

- Once four 90-day cycles have been completed and reviewed, an annual Value Assessment is carried out to look at progress over the longer term.

- Every 90-day cycle, you will start to see value being built into your three plans.

- Exit planning is a marathon, not a sprint. It requires commitment, discipline and Consistent action, which pays off in you and your business being prepared and protected for any eventuality.

PART TWO - THE METHODOLOGY

PHASE 4: COMPLETION

CHAPTER 16

Value Realisation

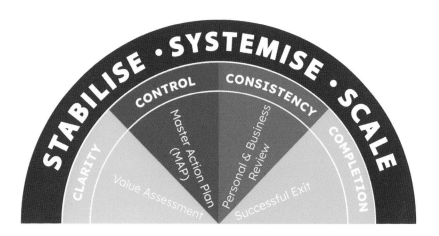

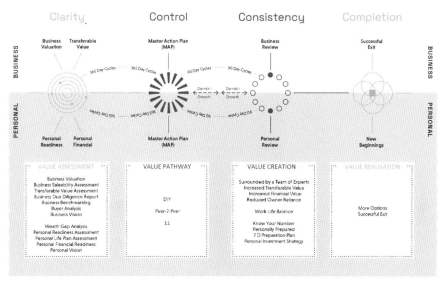

IN THE PREVIOUS chapters, you've come to understand that by having Clarity, you gain Control. Once you have Control, it is by Consistently working on your business using your Master Action Plan in a very systematic and focused way that you gain further Control. The more Control you gain and the more Consistent action you take, the closer you get to Completing your business, personal and financial goals and objectives. Completion refers to successfully exiting your business and realising all the value that has been created.

Value Realisation

At some point along your journey, you'll be confronted by one of the 7 Ds:
* Deal
* Decide
* Distress
* Disagreement
* Disease/Disability
* Divorce
* Death

When faced with one of the 7 Ds, you may need to exit your business – i.e., Completion – and all the work invested up to that point will come into play, allowing you to realise the value you have put in. Now that you are at the point of exit, be it forced or unforced, you'll be looking to embark on the next chapter of your life. You will now implement the procedures required to allow you to exit your business successfully.

Forced Exits

If you need to exit your business because life has thrown you a curveball, the policies and procedures you've put in place can now be implemented. Whatever the circumstance, trust the systems you have created and focus on yourself and your family. It is my sincere hope that no one reading this will need to take this route, but should this be the case, the actions you've taken up to this point should be enough to give you the options you need and, more importantly, the time and space to deal with the situation at hand.

Unforced Exits

During this phase, it will be important to remember that although you have consciously decided to leave the business, you have not left yet. A lot of owners get caught up in mentally checking out too soon. It is akin to a runner running a marathon and when they see the finish line 400 metres ahead, they stop running and go home. They did not Complete the race, and all the hard work they put in to get there they threw away before crossing the finishing line.

As an owner, you have not exited your business until the sale purchase agreement (SPA) has been signed or the planned liquidation has been completed. You must continue at the same level and pace as if you had decided to stay and grow the business. If the plan is to sell the business, between putting it on the market and signing the sale purchase agreement, a buyer will look for any downturn or change in trends within the business over and above the norm, and this will have an impact on valuation. So, you'll need to keep up with the great effort you have given thus far and push on until you have crossed the finish line. Only then have you reached Completion.

During the Completion phase, focus on the following areas:
- De-risking the business
- Starting the exit process
- Embarking on your new reality

De-Risking

The first step is to begin to make your business look as attractive as possible. Growing a business takes a lot of capital, and to do so may include taking on debt. Therefore, look to tidy up your balance sheet and pay off as much debt as possible, especially if there are any personal guarantees.

In order to speed up the due diligence process and make your business as attractive as possible, look to update your seller's pack. Your Business By Design advisor will have a template you can work from to create your own seller's pack.

Starting the Exit Process

At the same time, depending on which type of exit you decided upon at the start of this process, you will commence the sales or exit process.

Embarking on Your New Reality: Realising Your Vision

All this planning and implementation done at the beginning and during your 90-day cycles will now pay dividends. By planning what your life will look like once you leave your business, your vision will become your reality. Instead of having a feeling of dread and a loss of hope or identity, you will have a feeling of excitement and hope upon Completing your exit and realising your vision for your future.

This phase is the cumulation of the ups and downs of the journey that you embarked on all those years ago to finally reach your end goal, your destination. Of course, there may be a feeling of sadness and loss as with every life change, but by following this process, you'll be prepared for a life after your business from both a personal and financial point of view, which should make you very excited and confident to start your new chapter.

Let's return here to Bill, the business owner whose story I shared with you at the very start of this book. His dream was to sell his welding business, retire and relocate to the coast. But remember that he had not adequately prepared his business for sale. He was the key linchpin in his business and without him, his knowledge and his expertise, the business could not operate, leaving it unsaleable and his dreams for retirement unachievable. Now let's take a 'sliding doors' view and consider what his life may have been like had he followed the Business By Design methodology as set out across the chapters of this book. He would have gained a realistic view of his current business value and personal situation, enabling him to put steps in place to work towards his retirement goals. He would have de-risked his business, gradually withdrawing as the key linchpin and handing over the knowledge, skills and expertise through a strategic training programme, such as taking on apprentices to learn his craft. He would have become the CEO of his business, allocating the tasks associated with day-to-day running and production to others whilst working on growing the company, the business financials and finding and nurturing talent to take on his roles. In doing all this, he would have built a sustainable business with huge transferable value that could be sold, either internally or externally, and the legacy of his hard work and expertise would have continued. More significantly, Bill would have built sufficient value in his business through sensible wealth planning in order to fund the retirement plans he had so wished for. Unfortunately for Bill, he passed away whilst still working in his business and missed out on his dream of spending that precious time with his family.

I only wish I had been able to work with Bill much earlier in his business journey.

Chapter 16 Takeaways

- The final phase of the process is the Completion phase where you realise the value of your business through a successful exit.

  You will encounter one of the 7 Ds.

- If you encounter one of the 5 Ds that forces your exit, the plans, preparations and policies that have been put in place should still ensure that you exit successfully.

- If you have the option of planning an unforced exit (one of the last 2 Ds: deal and decide), you will set in motion the exit you have planned for.

- Don't forget that you have not exited your business until the sale purchase agreement has been signed or the liquidation is complete – don't 'check out' too soon!

- During the Completion phase you will focus on the following areas:
  - De-risking the business
  - Starting the exit process
  - Embarking on your new reality

- Consider Bill who, due to a lack of planning and preparation, was unable to sell his business and realise his retirement dreams. Don't be like Bill, or like the countless other business owners with whom I have had very similar encounters. Take Control of your future and make sure that you realise your dreams, whatever they may be.

Final Thoughts

IT IS MY SINCERE HOPE to see every owner exit their business successfully and realise the vision they had for their future when first starting out. If this methodology has made a difference to you, then I feel privileged and honoured to have played a small part in your journey.

I wish you every success in your entrepreneurial adventure.

About the Author

Working with business owners whose companies are at the early start-up phase right through to those with a multi-million pound turnover, Cliff focuses on a wide range of development areas: from organic growth, acquisitions and franchising/licensing, to constructing exit strategies for those business owners looking to retire or progress to other projects.

Outcomes are achieved by ensuring each business has the correct foundations in order to sustain growth in a controlled and organised manner. This includes training, working with staff and board members and creating coherence and focus to achieve the company's goals. In order to ensure a competitive edge, the company's finances, products/services, operations and future developments are analysed and developed to ensure maximum efficiency.

As an ex-military officer, Cliff gained valuable leadership and management skills. He has been trained to adapt and to seek effective solutions in an ever-changing environment. This has formed the backbone of his success in running his own companies for the past 20 years. Throughout this time, he has started, bought, sold, franchised, licensed and systematised several businesses in a variety of sectors.

To learn more about how Cliff could help you grow your business, as well as for more information and additional resources, please visit **www.businessbydesign.co.uk** or **www.thesmarterexit.com** or email **hello@businessbydesign.co.uk**.

Can You Help?

Thank You for Reading My Book!

I really appreciate all your feedback and I love hearing what you have to say.

I need your input to make the next version of this book and my future books even better.

Please leave me an honest review on Amazon, letting me know what you thought of the book, or you can email me at **hello@businessbydesign.co.uk**.

Thanks so much!

Cliff

Printed in Poland
by Amazon Fulfillment
Poland Sp. z o.o., Wrocław